Masala Dabba

Michael Swamy

Foreword: Dr. Manjit Singh Gill

Om Books International

Published in 2018 by

Om Books International

Corporate & Editorial Office
A-12, Sector 64, Noida 201 301
Uttar Pradesh, India
Phone: +91 120 477 4100
Email: editorial@ombooks.com
Website: www.ombooksinternational.com

Sales Office
107, Ansari Road, Darya Ganj, New Delhi 110 002, India
Phone: +91 11 4000 9000
Fax: +91 11 2327 8091
Email: sales@ombooks.com
Website: www.ombooks.com

Photography: Michael Swamy and Pravin Pol
Food Stylists: Michael Swamy and Mugdha Savkar
Recipe Trial: Ganesh Shedge
Back Cover Photograph: Ganesh Shedge
Research: Mrunal Savkar
Editor: Rita D'Souza
Design: Shraboni Roy

ISBN: 978-93-84225-63-6

Printed in India

10 9 8 7 6 5 4 3 2 1

For the teachers in my life,
Mum and Dad

I can no other answer make but thanks,
And thanks, and ever thanks.
—William Shakespeare

Contents

Foreword

Spices have always been the essence of our cooking and I am still learning.

The inspirational aromas of spices that drifted in from my mother's kitchen excited my senses and intrigued me to an extent to foray into the culinary world and train to be a chef.

Till today I spend endless hours trying to relearn the essence of each spice and clear the whiff of mystery that surrounds some of them. Some I have mastered and some still linger in the form of memories from my childhood.

I have always welcomed and encouraged chefs who have forayed into this vast subject, which will continue to surprise and further our knowledge in this science as I would like to coin it.

Today the cuisine of India is synonymous with the characteristics of our spices and understanding their best use. The world over, chefs are being inspired to cook and experiment with our "Masala Dabba".

Michael has done tremendous research and practiced the traditional dishes, and presented these dishes with his innovative thoughtful twists. It's all possible because of his skills and understanding of cookery. I am sure that this book will excite your palate just as much as it did mine and encourage your culinary talents and trysts on the stove.

I wish Michael all the best in this journey as a food writer and raise a toast to some happy and soulful cooking.

Dr. Manjit Singh Gill

Introduction

Indian food is synonymous with spice. The heady aroma that fills the air when a meal is being cooked, the hiss and splutter of spices and herbs as they hit the hot fat, leaching their oils and flavours into the seasoning, the sharp tingling on the tongue that awakens the taste buds, and the sight of a bright red curry or golden yellow shrikhand are as commonplace a phenomenon as they are a feast for the senses. The sights, sounds, smells and tastes of spices are so interwoven into India's culinary tapestry as to be impossible to imagine food anywhere in India without at least one spice infusing a dish with its magical charms.

The repository of all the kitchen magic that transforms a mundane offering into one that will set the senses singing is the masala dabba or the spice box. It has pride of place in every kitchen howsoever humble, always at the ready to offer up its contents of the most essential spices that flavour the family meal. And the rest are accommodated in containers of all shapes and sizes lining the kitchen shelves, within easy reach to create more magic by adding that little something special on their own, or in tandem with others.

India's romance with spices is as old as the country itself. The lush tropical forests of the south yielded the orbs of 'black gold' we call pepper, a treaure that countries waged war over and vied with each other to secure in what is now known as the age of discovery. It was in search of the precious black pepper that Europeans so coveted to flavour their meals, that Christopher Columbus ventured on an arduous ocean journey with the sole intention of locating India, the 'Land of Spices', and ended up discovering a new world on the other side of the globe altogether. He wasn't the only one—many more like him braved the untamed seas and traversed treacherous land routes in search of the aromatic ingredients. Indeed, it was this quest for spices that changed the history of the world, and India in particular, and moulded our culture into a melting pot of culinary traditions.

So integral is the chilli a part of Indian cooking that it may seem inconceivable that till a few hundred years ago it was unheard of on the Indian subcontinent, or for that matter anywhere in the East. The

Portuguese were responsible for introducing the chilli, which they brought from their colonies in South America and Africa. An introduction that has led to an everlasting bond: every regional cuisine —and India is blessed with many and varied culinary traditions—has the chilli as a prime ingredient.

But it does not stop with the chilli—which is just one of the many spices and herbs that flavour Indian cuisine. Indian food is known for the complexity and layers of flavour provided by the interplay of spices and herbs. Every region, every community has its own distinctive flavour notes which make it unique. Kashmiri Pandit cuisine has the delicate sweetness of fennel and dried ginger, while Kerala and other southern cuisines have the more robust flavours of peppercorns, cloves and cinnamon. In the East, mustard oils perfume a dish, while in the West, kokum adds tang and zing.

While geography, tradition, conquest and colonisation have played a role in shaping India's culinary profile as we know it today, Indian cuisine continues to evolve. New insights into the treatment of spices and other ingredients, new techniques and a great deal of imagination and daring have led to a whole new approach to Indian cooking. The traditional masala dabba has become a source of innovation, freeing chefs and home cooks from traditional practices to dare to combine flavours and textures in unconventional ways so traditional foods appear in new avatars, while always maintaining the essence of a dish.

In this new world of discovery and experimentation, the masala dabba is the springboard to adventure. You are invited to dissect and simplify flavours, developing a palate that discerns and understands the subtleties of each spice and flavouring, as well as the beauty of balance and harmony. And who knows—someday, you might just end up creating your own spice blend—a blend which defines not just your food, but your self too!

In this collection of recipes, I have done just that—used spices from the indispensable masala dabba and a variety of herbs to give an innovative twist to many traditional dishes. The familiar has been given a new dimension with an unusual, and if I may say so, a bold addition of herbs and spices, resulting in a marvellous mélange of flavours.

So go ahead, open up that masala dabba, reach for that bottle on the shelf and make some magic!

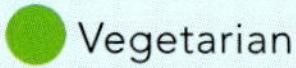

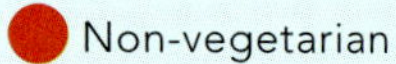

Spices, herbs and spice blends

Spices and herbs play a vital role in many cuisines around the world, more so in the cuisines of Southeast Asia and India. India has been both a producer and consumer of spices for thousands of years. Ancient Sanskrit texts emphasise their value as preservatives and as being rich in medicinal properties. Ayurveda, the ancient art of Hindu medicine, lists a whole range of herbs and spices for the cure of various ailments.

While modern-day use concerns itself mainly with flavour and taste, some therapeutic traditions remain. For instance, lentils and peas are cooked with a bit of ginger or asafoetida to counteract flatulence, or turmeric is mixed in hot milk to soothe a sore throat. Neem leaves are the answer to heal skin irritations and garlic is an excellent antiseptic.

There are no hard and fast rules concerning the use of spices and flavourings. Our taste buds, honed by tradition and experience, help us to choose which spices lend themselves to different aspects of cooking. Spices that are too strong or flavoursome are avoided in sweets; turmeric is used in small quantities and only in dishes that allow its flavour to mellow; and only a pinch of asafoetida is needed in a dish as its strong flavour is overpowering and can ruin a dish if burned. The choice of chillies depends on the colour and degree of hotness one prefers: dried red chillies, ground or powdered provide a mature heat, while green chillies add a fresh spiciness to a dish.

Buying and Storing Spices

In whichever way you decide to use spices or herbs, the first step is to buy the freshest and the best quality. Spices are best bought whole as berries, buds or bark. This allows the retention of flavour and their intrinsic pungency far longer than powdered spices.

Spices and herbs are at their flavoursome best in the summer months. In India, late summer is the ideal time for drying and preserving them and extracting their essential oils.

Spices like pepper, black cardamom or chillies are spread out on clean cloths and sun-dried till crisp. In some regions, a combination of spices is ground into a paste and dried in the form of small cakes to be stored for the whole year. The deep red Kashmiri veri masala is an example.

Herbs like mint, dill or coriander are washed and spread out to dry on clean cloths, in the shade, to prevent their blackening. Some herbs and aromatics like bay, ginger, onion, garlic and dill dry well if hung in small bunches in a warm, airy place away from direct sunlight.

The dried leaves, stems or pods need to be stored in airtight containers in a cool and dry area. However, it is important to note that dried herbs lose much of their flavour and one needs to use a larger amount when cooking.

A good way of keeping flavours of herbs and spices intact is by infusing them in oils and vinegars. These oils not only get concentrated with the flavours of the spice or herb but also make for excellent salad dressings or marinades.

Cooking with Spices and Herbs

While cooking, methods of preparation of spices, herbs and aromatics vary, all aimed at bringing out their maximum flavour. Every Indian kitchen uses several methods, some common to all, other methods used only in certain regions. An important tip to remember: spices and herbs are meant to flavour and not dominate a dish—so use them judiciously to create a harmony of tastes.

Dry-roasting: This is a process of heating a heavy-bottomed pan or griddle over low heat, then adding the spices and cooking them for a few seconds or up to a minute till fragrant; shaking the pan or tossing the spices continuously to prevent burning. The spices are then ground fine or pounded with a mortar and pestle.

Frying in fat: The pan is first heated, and the fat (usually oil or ghee) is added. When the fat is quite hot, the spices are added, immediately releasing their essential oils. At times, this method is used to infuse and flavour oils, where spices are removed from the oil after cooking.

Grating and chopping: This process is usually carried out for fresh ingredients like garlic, ginger and fresh turmeric root. Some spices like nutmeg are also grated before use.

Crushing: Bruising herbs and aromatics using the handle or flat blade of a knife helps release flavours of herbs like lemongrass, garlic and ginger. Tearing curry leaves before adding them to the pan also releases their flavour.

Grinding: A mortar and pestle and a grinding stone are common tools to pound or grind spices and herbs. Grinding releases oils, flavours and aromas. A few spices like dried ginger, cinnamon and turmeric are bought in the ground form, as they are hard to grind at home. Spices are best ground just before use or a day or two before.

Spice bags (potlis) and herb bundles (bouquet garni): Spice bags and herb bundles are used mostly when cooking rice dishes or stocks. Spices are tied together in a small bag using cheesecloth or muslin, and herbs are tied together in a bunch, and simmered in water or broth. This flavours the dish without one having to pick the spices or herbs out, which can be quite a cumbersome task.

Haldi
हल्दी
Rs 76/=
per

SPICE BLENDS

All the spices and herbs, previously described, are used either on their own or combined with others to make a blend. Though most blends are readily available in local grocery stores, it is easy to make them at home, and you experiment with proportions to create a tailor-made blend that appeals to specific taste. Given below are recipes for some blends that are often used.

Chaat Masala (Makes about ½ cup)

Available in most grocery stores, this is a versatile spice blend. An interesting piece of culinary history credits the creation of this blend to a hakim (medicine man) in Delhi, who used this combination of spices to treat and prevent digestive ailments. For a refreshing touch, try adding a teaspoon of dried mint while grinding.

Ingredients

½ tablespoon cumin seeds

½ tablespoon coriander seeds

1 heaped teaspoon dried pomegranate seeds (anardana)

1 teaspoon white peppercorns

¼ teaspoon carom seeds (ajwain)

½ teaspoon cloves

3 dried Kashmiri chillies

2½ tablespoons dried mango powder (amchur)

½ tablespoon coarse sea salt

½ tablespoon black salt

1 teaspoon asafoetida powder (hing)

Method

Heat a heavy-bottomed pan over low heat and separately dry-roast cumin seeds, coriander seeds, dried pomegranate seeds, white peppercorns, carom seeds, cloves and dried chillies. Cool to room temperature and combine with remaining ingredients in a spice grinder. Grind to a fine powder. Store in a clean, dry airtight container for up to 3 months in a cool, dry place away from sunlight.

Chhole Masala (Makes about ½ cup)

A spice blend used extensively in north India, particularly Punjab, this blend is specially reserved for a spicy, tangy chickpea curry which is enjoyed with hot fried breads at breakfast.

Ingredients

- 2 tablespoons cumin seeds
- 1 tablespoon caraway seeds (vilayati jeera)
- 4 - 5 dried red chillies
- 1 tablespoon coriander seeds
- ½ tablespoon black peppercorns
- 1 teaspoon cloves
- 1 tablespoon sesame seeds (til)
- 5 - 6 pods green cardamom
- 3 pods black cardamom
- 1 teaspoon turmeric powder
- 1 teaspoon dried ginger powder (sonth)
- 2 teaspoons dried mango powder (amchur)
- 4-inch cinnamon stick
- 2 medium bay leaves (tej patta)
- ½ teaspoon nutmeg powder (jaiphal)
- 1 heaped teaspoon powdered black salt

Method

Heat a heavy-bottomed pan over low heat and separately dry-roast cumin, caraway seeds, chillies, coriander seeds, black peppercorns, cloves, sesame seeds and green and black cardamom pods till they change colour slightly and are fragrant. Cool the roasted spices to room temperature and combine with remaining ingredients in a spice grinder. Grind to a fine powder and transfer to a clean, dry airtight jar. Store in a cool, dry and dark place for up to 3 months.

Curry Powder (Makes about ¾ cup)

Curry, in itself, is not a separate spice or dish. Derived from the Tamil word kari, curry refers to a sauce. It was the British who invented curry powder, which is a combination of ground spices they believed best replicated the curries and gravies they dined on during the Raj. Curry powder has a fairly standardised taste in the Western world, but in India, curry powder is available in many variations as every household and every region has its own version of the blend.

Ingredients

- ½ cup coriander seeds
- ⅓ cup cumin seeds
- 2 tablespoons turmeric powder
- ½ tablespoon green cardamoms
- 1 tablespoon cayenne pepper, paprika or mild
- 2 tablespoons Kashmiri chilli powder
- 1 tablespoon cloves
- ¼ teaspoon black peppercorns
- 1 tablespoon dried fenugreek leaves (kasuri methi)

Method

Combine all the spices. Using a spice grinder, grind the mixed spices in small batches to a fine powder. Alternatively, dry roast each ingredient, except turmeric and chilli powder, over low flame till fragrant. Then combine all spices and grind in a spice grinder to a fine powder. Transfer to a clean, dry glass jar and store in a cool, dry place.

Whole Garam Masala {Makes roughly 1 tablespoon (1 portion)}

Whole garam masala is a mix of whole spices that are generally used in seasoning or tempering (tadka), could be added to water while cooking rice or stocks for flavour and aroma. Use any combination of spices to suit your taste. The following is a basic recipe.

Ingredients

4 cloves

1-inch cinnamon stick

2 pods green cardamom

4 black peppercorns

1 large or 2 medium bay leaves (tej patta)

Method

Combine the whole spices together and use as required.

Other spices commonly used in whole garam masala mixtures are black cardamoms, dried red chillies, mace, star anise, cumin seeds and coriander seeds.

Paanch Phoran (Makes 1½ tablespoons)

This is a mix of 5 (paanch) spices used in equal proportions, found mainly in Bengali and Oriya cuisines. The whole spices can be mixed and stored in a clean, dry glass jar, ready for use.

Ingredients

1 teaspoon fennel seeds (saunf)

1 teaspoon nigella seeds (kalonji)

1 teaspoon fenugreek seeds (methi dana)

1 teaspoon cumin seeds

1 teaspoon black mustard seeds

Method

Combine the whole spices and use as required.

Though, the spices are usually mixed in equal proportions, the proportion of fenugreek may be reduced if one finds it too bitter. Other spices that can be used to lend an interesting touch to paanch phoran, as a substitute for any of the spices, are carom seeds (ajwain), brown mustard seeds, caraway seeds (vilayati jeera) and dill seeds (sowa).

Garam Masala Powder (Makes about 1/3 cup)

The most common spice blend used in Indian cooking, the recipe for garam masala powder differs from region to region and household to household. Given here is a basic recipe.

Ingredients

1 tablespoon black peppercorns

1 tablespoon cloves

2 teaspoons coriander seeds

1 teaspoon green cardamom pods

2 pods black cardamom

2 tablespoons cinnamon powder

2 large bay leaves (tej patta)

¼ teaspoon mace (javitri) powder

Method

Combine all the spices in a heavy-bottomed kadhai or wok; place on low heat and dry-roast, stirring constantly till spices change colour slightly and become very fragrant. Take care not to burn the spices. Remove from heat and continue stirring till mixture cools.

Alternatively, preheat oven to 150°C/300°F/Gas 2. Combine the spices on a large baking tray and roast for about 5 minutes, stirring occasionally. Take care not to burn the spices. Remove and cool to room temperature.

Grind in small batches, to a fine powder using a spice grinder. Fill into a clean, dry glass jar and store in a cool, dry place for up to 3 months.

Sambhar Masala

{Makes about 2 tablespoons (1 portion)}

Sambhar is a staple lentil dish in every south Indian home. Just like every other spice blend, this too is made differently in every home.

Ingredients

1 teaspoon oil

1 teaspoon split Bengal gram (chana dal)

1 teaspoon split white lentils (urad dal)

1 teaspoon fenugreek seeds (methi dana)

1 tablespoon coriander seeds

½ teaspoon cumin seeds

¼ teaspoon asafoetida powder (hing)

½ teaspoon turmeric powder

½ teaspoon black peppercorns

3 - 4 dried red chillies

Method

Heat oil in a frying pan; add split Bengal gram, white lentils and fenugreek seeds and fry over low heat till golden. Add the remaining ingredients and fry till spices are golden in colour and a strong aroma fills the air. Remove from heat, cool and grind to a coarse powder.

Pavbhaji Masala (Makes about ½ cup)

This is a famous Mumbai spice blend that gives the iconic street snack its flavour. Even today, when one walks on Mumbai streets late at night, one cannot escape the aroma of this blend as it cooks with crushed tomatoes and vegetables on large griddles by the roadside.

Ingredients

5 tablespoons coriander seeds

2 tablespoons cumin seeds

1 tablespoon black peppercorns

½ teaspoon fenugreek seeds (methi dana)

2 pods black cardamom

6 - 7 cloves

2-inch cinnamon stick

1 tablespoon chilli powder (deggi mirch)

1 teaspoon turmeric powder

1 tablespoon dried mango powder (amchur)

¼ teaspoon grated nutmeg (jaiphal)

2 teaspoons dried fenugreek leaves (kasuri methi), powdered

1 teaspoon black salt

Method

Combine whole spices in a pan and dry-roast over medium-low heat till very fragrant. Cool to room temperature and combine in a spice grinder with remaining spices.

Grind to a fine powder and transfer to a clean, dry glass jar. Store in a cool and dry place for up to 3 months.

Meat Masala (Makes about ½ cup)

Mostly used in combination with garam masala, meat masala can be used in curries as well as a marinade. In some households, it is also combined with tamarind pulp to make a spice paste.

Ingredients

1 tablespoon vegetable oil

5 tablespoons coriander seeds

3 tablespoons fennel seeds (saunf)

2 tablespoons black peppercorns

8 dried red chillies

4-inch cinnamon stick

2 pods black cardamom

4 pods green cardamom

2 star anise (chakri phool/badiyan)

1 teaspoon cloves

Method

Heat oil in a pan over low heat and separately fry each spice till it changes colour slightly and is very fragrant. Cool to room temperature and grind to a fine powder using a spice grinder. Transfer to a clean, dry jar and store in a cool dry place for up to 1 month.

Fish Masala (Makes about ¾ cup)

Fish masala is a common spice blend in many coastal homes. One can substitute Byadgi chillies with any other variety depending on how spicy one likes the blend.

Ingredients

2 tablespoons vegetable oil
10 - 12 dried red Byadgi chillies
2 tablespoons coriander seeds
1 tablespoon fennel seeds (saunf)
1 small blade mace (javitri)
1½ tablespoons poppy seeds (khus khus)
2-inch cinnamon stick
1 teaspoon black peppercorns
½ teaspoon cloves
1 teaspoon cumin seeds
½ teaspoon cobra saffron (nagkesar)
1 heaped teaspoon black mustard seeds
2 large bay leaves (tej patta)
2 pieces stone flower (dagad phool)
½ teaspoon tirphal
2 pods black cardamom
3 pods green cardamom
1 teaspoon turmeric powder
A tiny piece of asafoetida

Method

Heat oil in a heavy-bottomed pan over low heat and roast each spice separately till fragrant. Cool to room temperature and grind to a fine powder using a spice grinder. Transfer to a clean, dry airtight jar and add a small piece of asafoetida to the jar. Store in a cool, dry place for up to 4 months.

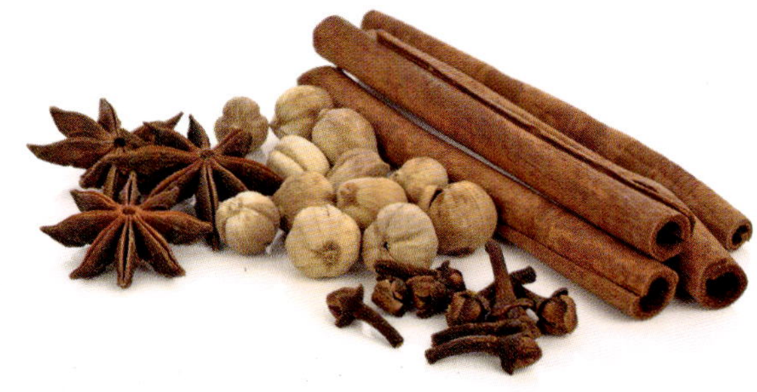

Kitchen King Masala (Makes about ¾ cup)

A popular spice blend, kitchen king masala is a versatile mix of spices that can be used in any curry.

Ingredients

2 tablespoons split Bengal gram (chana dal)

1 tablespoon cumin seeds

1 tablespoon coriander seeds

1 tablespoon fennel seeds (saunf)

½ tablespoon caraway seeds (vilayati jeera)

½ tablespoon black peppercorns

½ tablespoon yellow mustard seeds

8 cloves

8 dried red chillies

2 teaspoons fenugreek seeds (methi dana)

3 pods black cardamom

6 pods green cardamom

3-inch cinnamon stick

1 large blade mace (javitri)

1 teaspoon turmeric powder

½ tablespoon dried ginger powder (sonth)

Method

Separately dry-roast each ingredient, except turmeric and dried ginger powder, in a heavy-bottomed pan over low heat. Transfer to a spice grinder, add turmeric and ginger powder and grind to a fine powder. Store in a clean, dry airtight container for up to 3 months.

Dhansak Masala (Makes about ½ cup)

Dhansak is always associated with Parsis. Though a dish made during days of mourning, over time, it has become a regular feature at Sunday lunch in Parsi homes. Traditionally, the women of the household would grind the masala fresh and cook the dhansak over low heat over 4 or 5 hours. Today, several commercial versions of the blend are readily available, but this home-made one makes it extra special.

Ingredients

4-inch cinnamon stick

1 tablespoon coriander seeds

½ tablespoon green cardamom pods

3 pods black cardamom

1½ tablespoons black peppercorns

2 large bay leaves (tej patta)

2 teaspoons cloves

1½ teaspoons caraway seeds (vilayati jeera)

1 teaspoon cumin seeds

2 star anise (chakri phool/badiyan)

1 teaspoon fennel seeds (saunf)

1 teaspoon brown mustard seeds

½ teaspoon fenugreek seeds (methi dana)

1 whole small nutmeg (jaiphal), broken into small pieces

Method

Combine all ingredients in a heavy-bottomed pan and dry-roast over a medium-low heat till very fragrant. Transfer to a spice grinder and grind to a fine powder. Store for up to 6 months in a clean, dry glass jar, away from sunlight.

Pickle Masala (Makes 1½ tablespoons)

The combination of pickling spices differs from region to region. Some use an elaborate mix of spices and herbs, while others use a brine solution with just one or two flavourings. For a quick mix, you can either use any pickling blend containing mustard and red chillies, or make your own.

Ingredients

2 teaspoons red chilli powder

1 teaspoon mustard powder

½ teaspoon fenugreek (methi) powder

½ teaspoon turmeric powder

¼ teaspoon asafoetida powder

Method

Combine all the spice powders and use as required.

Milk Masala (Makes about 1½ tablespoons)

This is a spice blend used to make a warm milk concoction in winter, especially in north India. Masala milk is a comforting beverage packed with nutrients guaranteed to lift one's spirits on a dreary day.

Ingredients

1 teaspoon melon seeds (char magaz)

4 - 6 almonds

½ teaspoon poppy seeds (khus khus)

¼ teaspoon fennel seeds (saunf)

1 teaspoon saffron strands

Seeds of 4 green cardamom pods

Method

Lightly dry-roast the melon seeds, almonds, poppy seeds and fennel seeds in a pan and cool to room temperature.

Add the saffron and cardamom seeds, and crush in a mortar and pestle to make a coarse powder.

SOUPS

While soups are not often associated with Indian cuisine, the truth is there is a variety of hot and cold beverages that make for perfect soups. Shorbas, rasams, lentil broths and light gravies, served at the start or during the course of a meal, play the role of a soup, which is to refresh and activate the taste buds.

A soup or broth will only be as good as the stock that forms the base of the beverage. The freshest ingredients of the best quality play an integral role in giving a soup its body and character. Before cooking, vegetables and lentils should be washed well, and the bones and carcass of poultry or meat should be washed and roasted in an oven before boiling for best results. Add a bouquet garni (bundle of herbs) and whole spices tied up in a bundle, and aromatics like onion to provide flavour. As the broth boils, skim it frequently to remove the frothy scum and other impurities, and cook it on the gentlest heat for a clear, flavourful stock.

Spices and herbs used in soups should be light and simple. Strong flavours will not only kill the flavour of the soup, but put one off the rest of the meal. Spices like pepper, star anise, and hints of clove and cinnamon are ideal. Too many spices will turn a soup into a curry, so choose your spices and flavouring with care.

Baingan Ka Shorba

बैंगन का शोरबा

Roasted Eggplant Soup

Serves 4 - 6

As a child I loved baingan ka bharta (spicy eggplant mash). And soup has always been my favourite comfort food. So, I decided to combine the two by incorporating some new flavours and came up with this lip-smacking brinjal soup!

Ingredients

3 large eggplants
18 large cloves garlic, peeled
6 sprigs fresh rosemary or 1 tablespoon dried rosemary
4 tablespoons olive oil
4 cups vegetable stock
2 tablespoons butter
3 medium onions, finely chopped
1 teaspoon cumin powder
1 teaspoon black pepper powder
½ cup cream
Salt to taste

Method

- Stud each eggplant with 4 cloves of garlic and 2 sprigs of rosemary. Finely chop the remaining garlic.
- Brush the eggplants with olive oil and roast over an open flame, turning regularly to ensure even roasting and cooking. When cooked through, remove from heat and cool.
- Peel the eggplants, chop the flesh roughly and pass through a sieve to get a smooth purée. Alternatively, blend to a smooth purée with some stock and strain the purée.
- Heat remaining olive oil with butter in a large saucepan; add chopped garlic with onions and sauté till translucent.
- Stir in eggplant purée, sauté for 2 to 3 minutes, then add the remaining vegetable stock and whisk the soup till smooth. Add cumin powder and pepper powder and bring the soup to a boil.
- Stir in cream and salt, cook for 1 more minute, and serve hot with breadsticks.

Kaddu Ka Rasam

कद्दू का रसम

Spiced Pumpkin Broth

Serves 6 – 8

My dad being a South Indian, rasam (spicy, flavourful soup made from the broth derived from cooking lentils) was a regular feature at dinner. Mum being East Indian, pumpkin foogath was the other regular one. This recipe brings together the flavours and contrasting textures of both in one satisfying bowl.

Ingredients

2 tablespoons butter

2 large onions, finely sliced

1 small pumpkin (about 750 gm) (kaddu), peeled and diced

8 - 9 cloves garlic

4 sprigs fresh rosemary or

1 tablespoon dried rosemary

2 heaped teaspoons rasam powder (See NOTE below)

8 cups lentil, vegetable or chicken stock

Salt to taste

Black pepper powder to taste

Method

- Heat butter in a large saucepan over medium heat. When butter melts, add onions and sauté till translucent.
- Add pumpkin, garlic and rosemary and sauté till the pumpkin softens.
- Mix in rasam powder, sauté for a minute, then stir in 6 cups stock, salt and pepper and bring the mixture to a boil.
- When pumpkin is cooked, remove mixture from heat, cool to room temperature and blend till smooth in a blender. Strain into the same saucepan with remaining stock.
- Reheat the soup till it simmers and serve hot with garlic bread.

NOTE: Rasam powder is easily available in most grocery stores. However, you can easily make your own rasam powder at home. Combine 3 heaped teaspoons cumin seeds, 1½ teaspoons coriander seeds, 2 teaspoons peppercorns, 2 large sprigs fresh curry leaves, and 4 to 6 dried red chillies in a heavy-bottomed pan and dry-roast over medium-low heat till very fragrant. Cool the spices and grind to a fine powder with ½ teaspoon asafoetida powder. Use as specified in the recipe and store the rest in an airtight container.

Ananas Badam Soup

Chilled Pineapple And Almond Soup

अनानास बादाम सूप

Serves 4 - 6

Ingredients

2 large ripe fresh pineapples, diced
5 - 6 cups water
1 teaspoon dried ginger powder (sonth)
½ teaspoon white pepper powder
½ cup almonds, blanched and peeled
1 cup skimmed milk
Salt to taste
1 dried red chilli, cut into slivers for garnish (optional)
6 - 8 rose petals, for garnish (optional)

The pineapples of southern India are a delight! This fat-free soup couples the weight-reducing properties of pineapple and dried ginger with the subtle richness of almonds to make a dessert-like soup. An ideal weight-watcher's soup!

Method

- Combine the pineapples with 5 to 6 cups water, ginger powder and white pepper powder in a saucepan and place over medium-high heat. Bring to a boil, reduce the heat and simmer for 5 minutes till the pineapple is pulpy. Remove from heat and cool to room temperature.
- Meanwhile, combine almonds with milk in a blender and purée till smooth. Add the cooled pineapple mixture with the liquid and blend till smooth.
- Strain into a large bowl, mix in salt and refrigerate to chill.
- Ladle into individual bowls, garnish with chilli slivers and rose petals. Serve.

Smoked Tamatar Shimla Mirch Soup Cheese Ke Saath

स्मोक्ड टमाटर शिमला मिर्च सूप चीज़ के साथ

Chilli-smoked Tomato Pepper Soup With Cheese

Serves 4 - 6

I created this recipe for the 6th Street Café, I once ran in Pune. The food, look and feel of the restaurant was French, so I brought all the favourite French ingredients together in a bowl with a hint of spice.

Ingredients

- 2 medium red capsicums
- 2 medium green capsicums
- 4 medium tomatoes
- 1 teaspoon vegetable oil
- 2 tablespoons butter
- 1 large onion, roughly chopped
- 4 cloves garlic, roughly chopped
- 1 teaspoon black pepper powder
- 1 teaspoon red chilli powder
- ½ cup tomato purée
- 2 - 3 cups vegetable or chicken stock
- Rock salt to taste
- ¾ cup grated cheese
- 2 tablespoons cream
- 1 teaspoon chaat masala (See page 17)
- A few sprigs of chives, to garnish (optional)

Method

- Lightly brush the capsicums and tomatoes with oil and with the help of tongs roast each one over an open flame. When the vegetables are evenly charred, cool to room temperature and scrape off the charred peel with a knife. Roughly chop the roasted vegetables.
- Heat butter in a large saucepan over medium heat. When the butter melts, add onion and garlic and sauté till translucent.
- Add chopped roasted vegetables and sauté for 5 to 6 minutes till mixture is very fragrant. Stir in the pepper, chilli powder and tomato purée. Stir in 1½ cups stock and salt and bring the soup to a boil. Remove from heat; cool to room temperature and purée the soup in a blender till smooth.
- Strain the purée into the same saucepan used before, and reheat the soup over medium heat. If the soup is too thick for your liking, stir in some more stock.
- When the soup is hot, reduce heat to low and stir in the cheese. DO NOT ALLOW THE SOUP TO BOIL. As soon as the cheese melts, stir in cream and immediately remove the soup from heat.
- Ladle the soup into 4 to 6 bowls and sprinkle ¼ teaspoon chaat masala on top. Serve hot, garnished with chives.

Chukander Ka Shorba

चुकंदर का शोरबा

Roasted Beetroot Soup

Serves 4 - 6

The luscious, dark fuchsia colour, and warm sweet flavour of beetroot makes me wonder why everyone is so partial to tomato soup. Whether sweet or not, the beetroot makes for an excellent soup vegetable, and hints of Indian spice make it even more flavourful.

Ingredients

1 large white radish, peeled and sliced
3 large beetroots, peeled and sliced
1 large carrot, peeled and sliced
8 shallots, peeled and tops cut off
1 large sprig fresh curry leaves
½ teaspoon black peppercorns
1 teaspoon cumin seeds
4 large cloves garlic
1 tablespoon olive oil
2 medium tomatoes, sliced
3 cups vegetable stock
Sea salt to taste
2 tablespoons cream

FOR CHILLI OIL
2 tablespoons vegetable oil
1 tablespoon red chilli powder

FOR CURRY LEAF SEASONING
1 tablespoon vegetable oil
1 small sprig fresh curry leaves
½ teaspoon cumin seeds

Method

- Preheat oven to 150°C/300°F/Gas 2.
- Line a baking tray with foil and spread the prepared radish, beetroot, carrot and shallots on it. Mix well and sprinkle curry leaves, peppercorns, cumin seeds and garlic over the vegetables. Drizzle over with olive oil and roast in the oven for 15 minutes till the vegetables soften slightly.
- Mix the sliced tomatoes with the roasting vegetables and roast for 5 more minutes. When the vegetables soften, remove from oven and cool to room temperature.
- Combine vegetables with 1½ cups vegetable stock in a blender and purée till smooth. Strain the soup through a fine strainer; mix in the remaining stock and heat. Add sea salt.
- To make the chilli oil, heat oil in a small frying pan over medium heat and add chilli powder. Cook for 5 seconds, remove from heat and cool. Strain the oil into a bowl.
- For the curry leaf seasoning, heat oil in a small frying pan over medium heat. Add the curry leaves and cumin seeds. Cook till the cumin crackles and curry leaves are crisp. Remove from heat.
- To serve, ladle soup into soup plates or bowls; drizzle over with cream, chilli oil and fried curry leaf seasoning. Serve immediately.

Summer Shorba

समर शोरबा

Serves 4

A shorba is a thin well-flavoured soup. I first created this soup for a gourmet summit in Singapore a couple of years ago, and the original recipe contained a variety of exotic vegetables and edible flowers. However, I realised that the simpler version with everyday vegetables tastes just as good. Simply reduce the amount of spice paste for a milder soup.

Ingredients

FOR BROTH

- 2 large onions, roughly sliced
- 6 cloves garlic, roughly chopped
- 1-inch piece ginger, roughly chopped
- 3 whole dried red chillies
- ¼ cup water
- 1 tablespoon oil
- 2 fresh lemongrass stalks
- 1 tablespoon sambhar masala (See page 20)
- 1 teaspoon turmeric powder or 2 teaspoons fresh turmeric paste
- 1 cup coconut milk
- 3 cups vegetable or chicken stock
- Salt to taste

FOR VEGETABLES

- 6 - 8 button mushrooms, quartered
- 1 cup large tofu cubes, cut into fine strips
- ½ cup American corn kernels, steamed
- 1 medium cucumber, cut into fine strips
- 2 stalks spring onion greens, finely sliced
- 1 medium carrot, peeled and cut into fine strips
- ¼ cup assorted edible flowers (such as marigold petals, dried rose petals), to garnish

Method

- For the broth, combine the onions, garlic, ginger and red chillies in a blender with ¼ cup water and blend to a smooth paste.
- Heat oil in a large kadhai over medium heat. Crush the lemongrass with the back of a wooden spoon and add to the oil. When the oil sizzles, add the ground paste and sauté for a minute.
- Add sambhar masala, turmeric powder or paste and 2 tablespoons water and continue to sauté till fragrant.
- Add coconut milk, stock and salt and bring to a boil, stirring continuously.
- Reduce the heat to low and add all the ingredients required for the vegetable mixture, except flowers, and simmer for 5 minutes.
- Serve hot, garnished with edible flowers.

STARTERS AND SNACKS

Starters and snacks are an integral part of an Indian meal. Earlier, small crisp bites would be served along with the rest of the meal in a thali. Now that our patterns of dining have undergone a change, small, savoury titbits are served before a meal, usually accompanied by beverages.

Snacks become the main event at cocktail parties, tea parties and other informal events where no main meal is to follow. Indian snacks are either fried, baked or steamed and their variety is endless: from light, spongy square dhoklas, to hefty, corpulent vada pavs and crisp chivdas and namkeen, there is no dearth of small eats and munchies to delight the palate. Almost any spice or herb can be used to perk up a snack, and the spicy, herby chutneys and sauces that are served with these savoury mouthfuls only add to the pleasure.

Aloo Matar Tikki Aur Kurkuri Bhindi (Potato And Pea Patties With Okra Crisps)

Chukander Galauti Kebab (Melt-in-mouth Beetroot Kebabs)

Bombay Toast

Masaledar Sabzi Chips (Spicy Root Vegetable Chips)

Tandoori Chicken Liver Pâté

Goat Cheese Pakoda Cherry Tamatar Salad Ke Saath
(Fried Goat Cheese Balls With Cherry Tomato Salad)

Aloo Matar Tikki Aur Kurkuri Bhindi

आलू मटर टिक्की और कुरकुरी भिंडी

Potato And Pea Patties With Okra Crisps

Makes 8 - 10 tikkis

On my way home from school, hungry and tired, salvation was provided by the corner chaatwala who would be frying crisp, fat aloo tikkis on a huge black griddle, which he served with tangy curried peas. These tikkis are equally satisfying, especially paired with crisp deep-fried okra.

Ingredients

FOR TIKKI

- 1 tablespoon oil, plus for shallow-frying
- ½ teaspoon nigella (kalonji)
- 1 tablespoon ginger-garlic paste
- 1 cup fresh or frozen peas
- 1 teaspoon garam masala (See page 20)
- ½ teaspoon dried mango powder (amchur)
- Salt to taste
- 4 large potatoes, boiled, peeled and mashed well
- ¼ teaspoon powdered sugar

FOR OKRA CRISPS

- 8 - 10 okra (bhindi), washed, dried well and finely sliced
- 2 tablespoons rice flour
- ½ teaspoon white pepper powder
- Salt to taste
- Vegetable oil for deep-frying

Method

- For tikki, heat oil in a frying pan over medium heat. Add nigella and when they crackle, add ginger-garlic paste and peas, and sauté till the peas are tender and very fragrant.
- Add garam masala, mango powder and salt, and cook for 2 to 3 minutes more. Remove from heat and cool to room temperature.
- In a mixing bowl, combine mashed potatoes with salt and sugar and mix well. Divide the mixture into lime-sized portions.
- To shape the tikki, grease your palms and flatten one portion of potato mixture on your palm. Place a teaspoonful of pea mixture in the centre. Carefully bring the potato mixture together to enclose the peas completely. Repeat with the remaining potato and pea mixture.
- Heat a griddle or frying pan over medium-low heat and grease well. Place the prepared tikki on the pan and shallow-fry on both sides; drizzle oil till golden and crisp. Remove and drain on absorbent paper.
- For okra crisps, toss okra in a mixture of rice flour, pepper and salt.
- Heat oil in a kadhai or wok over medium-high heat till a piece of okra added to it sizzles and comes to the surface. Add the okra and deep-fry till crisp. Drain on absorbent paper.
- Garnish the tikki with okra crisps and serve with chutney.

Chukander Galauti Kebab

चुकंदर गलौती कबाब

Melt-in-mouth Beetroot Kebabs

Makes 8 - 10 kebabs

As I wandered through the streets of Lucknow, I came upon a man making vegetarian Galauti Kebabs from minced cauliflower. I tasted one and decided to give the famous meaty Tunday Kebabs a miss! Here, I have used the sweetness of beetroot coupled with spices to make delicious, melt-in-mouth kebabs.

Ingredients

3 large beetroots, peeled, grated and moisture squeezed out
1 heaped teaspoon ginger paste
1 heaped teaspoon garlic paste
½ teaspoon carom seeds (ajwain)
Salt to taste
Black pepper powder to taste
½ teaspoon garam masala (See page 20)
2 tablespoons chironjee (Calumpong nuts), soaked in hot water for 30 minutes
1 egg (optional)
½ cup fresh breadcrumbs
Vegetable oil for shallow-frying

TO SERVE

2 large onions, finely sliced and soaked in ⅓ cup vinegar for 2 hours
Raita or yoghurt (optional)

Method

- In a blender or processor, combine beetroot with ginger paste, garlic paste, carom seeds, salt, pepper, garam masala powder and drained chironjee. Grind to a smooth fine paste.
- Transfer the mixture to a strainer lined with muslin or cheesecloth and set aside for 30 minutes till extra moisture drains away.
- Transfer this mixture to a bowl and add egg and breadcrumbs. Mix well and divide the mixture into lime-sized portions. Shape each portion into a flat round patty.
- Heat a griddle or frying pan over medium heat and brush liberally with oil. Place the patties on the pan and shallow-fry on both sides; drizzle oil till golden and cooked through. Remove and drain on absorbent paper.
- To serve, drain the vinegar from onions. Serve hot beetroot kebabs with vinegar onions and raita or yoghurt.

Bombay Toast

Serves 6 - 8

Ingredients

6 large eggs
Salt to taste
Black pepper powder to taste
Red chilli powder to taste
½ teaspoon cumin powder
2 tablespoons dried fenugreek leaves (kasuri methi)
1 heaped teaspoon pickle masala (See page 25)
¼ cup grated cheese
½ cup finely chopped fresh coriander leaves
8 large slices multigrain bread
Vegetable oil for deep-frying

This dish is inspired by an Anglo-Indian recipe for savoury French toast. The original dish is made by dipping plain, sliced white bread in beaten eggs and frying it crisp. Here, I've used multigrain bread and added spices and herbs to the eggs to make for a wholesome breakfast or teatime snack.

Method

- In a large mixing bowl, whisk eggs with all the ingredients except bread slices and oil.
- Heat oil in a kadhai or wok over medium heat till a drop of egg batter added to it sizzles and rises to the surface.
- Dip each slice of bread in the prepared egg batter, add to the oil and deep-fry till golden and crisp. Remove and drain on absorbent paper.
- Serve hot with a sauce or chutney.

Masaledar Sabzi Chips

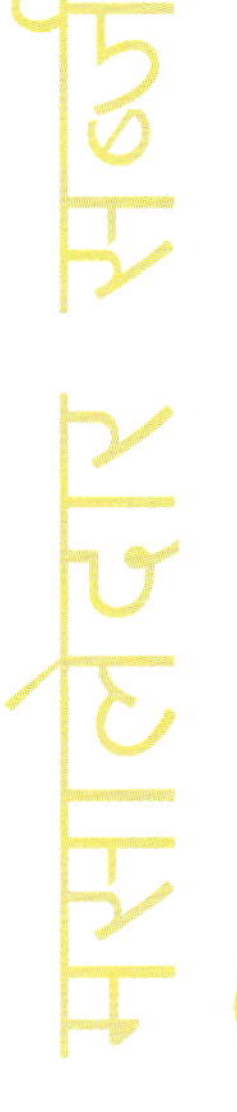

Spicy Root Vegetable Chips

Serves 4

Ingredients

2 lotus stems (kamal kakdi)

2 medium sweet potatoes

200 g yam (jimikand)

2 medium-thick carrots, peeled and finely sliced

2 medium beetroots, peeled and finely sliced

½ cup rice flour

1 teaspoon red chilli powder

Salt to taste

Vegetable oil for deep-frying

2 teaspoons chaat masala (See page 17)

I first made these chips in Kuwait where I used to work as a menu-planning officer. Fed up with the daily dose of potato chips, I once sneaked into the kitchen and made chips from whatever vegetables I could lay my hands on. And ever since then, we stopped eating potato chips!

Method

- Peel the lotus stems, sweet potatoes and yam; slice finely and soak in the salted water for 20 minutes. Drain and pat dry with a clean kitchen towel.
- Combine with carrots, beetroots, rice flour, chilli powder and salt in a large mixing bowl and mix well.
- Heat oil in a kadhai or wok over medium-high heat till a small slice of carrot added to it sizzles and rises to the surface. Add spiced vegetables to the hot oil in batches and deep-fry till golden and crisp. Remove and drain on absorbent paper.
- Transfer to a bowl, sprinkle chaat masala and toss well. Serve immediately.

Tandoori Chicken Liver Pâté

तन्दूरी चिकन लिवर पाते

Serves 4 - 6

Ingredients

1½ cups plain yoghurt

2 teaspoons ginger-garlic paste

1 tablespoon mustard oil

¾ teaspoon red chilli powder

¾ teaspoon nigella seeds (kalonji)

Juice of 1 lime

Salt to taste

Black pepper powder to taste

250 g chicken liver, cleaned and cut into ½-inch cubes

½ cup butter

TO SERVE

Whole wheat crackers

At Le Cordon Bleu, we were once asked to innovate on the classic French pâté. I thought, why not add tandoori spices! Twenty years later, I think I should have smoked the pâté to give it the taste of the tandoor.

Method

- In a mixing bowl, combine yoghurt with ginger-garlic paste, mustard oil, chilli powder, nigella seeds, lime juice, salt and pepper. Whisk well. Add the chicken liver and set aside to marinate for 30 to 45 minutes.
- Heat a frying pan over medium heat; add the chicken liver with marinade and butter, and cook stirring continuously for 6 to 7 minutes or till the chicken liver is done. Remove from heat and cool to room temperature.
- Transfer the mixture to a food processor or blender and blend till the mixture is very smooth and fluffy.
- Pour into pâté moulds or small jars and chill till set.
- Serve with whole wheat crackers or use as a sandwich filling.

Goat Cheese Pakoda Cherry Tamatar Salad Ke Saath

गोट चीज़ पकोड़ा टमाटर सलाद के साथ

Fried Goat Cheese Balls With Cherry Tomato Salad

Makes 8 - 10 cheese balls

This South American favourite goes well with Indian spices. The ripeness of the cheese absorbs the flavours of the spices, adding a little tang and a sharp bite. Cheeses have come a long way now with home-styled cheeses being made in India.

Ingredients

1 tablespoon vegetable oil, plus for deep-frying
1 medium onion, finely chopped
6 cloves garlic, finely chopped
2 green chillies, deseeded and finely chopped
4 - 5 large button mushrooms, finely chopped
200 g goat cheese, crumbled or grated
Salt to taste
Black pepper powder to taste
½ teaspoon cumin powder
1 teaspoon dried mango powder (amchur)
1 egg, lightly beaten
½ cup semolina (sooji)
½ cup all-purpose flour (maida)

FOR CHERRY TOMATO SALAD
5 - 7 cherry tomatoes, halved
1 medium onion, finely sliced
1 tablespoon balsamic vinegar
Salt to taste
Black pepper powder to taste

Method

- Heat 1 tablespoon oil in a medium frying pan over medium heat. Add onion, garlic and green chillies. Sauté for a few seconds.
- Add the mushrooms and sauté till the onions and mushrooms are soft. Remove from heat and cool slightly.
- Add goat cheese, salt, pepper, cumin powder, mango powder and egg. Divide the mixture into lime-sized portions. Roll each portion into a ball.
- Combine semolina and flour in a plate and mix well. Roll the cheese balls in the semolina-flour mixture to coat evenly.
- Heat oil in a kadhai or wok over medium heat till tiny bubbles appear on the base. Carefully add 3 or 4 cheese balls at a time and deep-fry till golden and crisp. Remove and drain on absorbent paper.
- For the salad, combine cherry tomatoes, onion, balsamic vinegar, salt and pepper in a mixing bowl and toss well.
- Serve hot fried cheese balls with salad.

EGGS

My childhood fascination with eggs was not so much eating them at home, but witnessing a street vendor selling boiled eggs, sprinkled liberally with chilli powder. It seemed to me then that eggs could do well with a dash of spice to liven up their blandness and I was right. You will find eggs in various avatars in kitchens across India: scrambled with herbs and spices, single or double-fried, sprinkled with pepper, whole or half-boiled eggs swimming in curries; whisked into Indian Chinese soups, smeared with fresh herbs, onions and tomatoes in colourful omelettes, and if Parsis are to be believed, eggs sizzling atop spiced vegetables and meats taste divine!

Anokhe Nargisi Kofte

अनोखे नरगीसी कोफ्ते

Soft-centred Scotch Eggs

Serves 3 - 4

Ingredients

5 eggs
500 g minced lamb
2 teaspoons meat masala (See page 21)
Salt to taste
2 tablespoons cornflour
1 cup all-purpose flour (maida)
1 cup fresh breadcrumbs
Vegetable oil for deep-frying

The Scotch egg is believed to have originated in Mughal India where it was known as Nargisi Kofta. Though both versions use a hard-boiled egg, I decided to use soft-boiled eggs instead. To achieve this, it's important to remember not to let the eggs boil for more than 3 minutes, or else the yolk will harden, and you will be deprived of the pleasure of seeing a silken ribbon of golden yolk flow out of the egg when halved.

Method

- Place 4 eggs in a saucepan filled three-fourth with water and place over medium-high heat. Bring the water to a boil, constantly stirring the eggs. Allow the eggs to boil for 3 minutes, then drain and place in a bowl filled with ice water. Leave to cool for 2 minutes.
- Carefully peel the soft-boiled eggs and set aside.
- Combine the minced lamb/beef with meat masala, salt and cornflour in a food processor and grind to a smooth paste. Divide into 4 equal portions.
- Spread a piece of cling film on a chopping board and place one portion of mince mixture on it. Using the back of a spoon, spread the mixture slightly and place a soft-boiled egg on it. Carefully gather the cling film around the egg so that it is completely covered with mince. Bring the edges of the cling film together and twist gently to seal the egg within the mince. Repeat with the remaining mixture and soft-boiled eggs.
- Spread flour and breadcrumbs on separate plates. Lightly beat the remaining raw egg.
- Remove one mince-covered egg from the cling film and carefully roll it in the flour, giving it a proper egg shape while doing so. Dip the mince-covered egg in the beaten egg and roll in breadcrumbs, coating evenly on all sides. Set aside and repeat with the remaining eggs.

- Preheat oven to 180˚C/350°F/Gas 4.
- Heat oil in a kadhai or wok over medium heat till a pinch of breadcrumbs added to it sizzle. Place a crumbed egg on a perforated spoon and carefully lower it into the hot oil. Deep-fry till golden and crisp. Remove, drain on absorbent paper and place on a baking tray lined with foil. Repeat with the remaining eggs.
- Cover the fried mince-coated eggs with another piece of foil and bake in the preheated oven for 10 minutes.
- Remove from the oven and cut each egg in half—the yolk should be liquid and should ooze out. Serve immediately with salad.

Fried Eggs Ke Saath Teekha Rajma

फ्राइड एग्स के साथ तीखा राजमा

Fried Eggs With Chilli Beans

Serves 4

From Goa comes this breakfast dish of curried black-eyed beans, which I have substituted with kidney beans. The curry has been turned into a spicy sauce to be served with silky fried eggs. Eat it with toast for a complete meal to start your day.

Ingredients

FOR CHILLI BEANS

1 tablespoon butter

½ teaspoon nigella seeds (kalonji), crushed

½ teaspoon fennel seeds (saunf), lightly toasted and crushed

1 tablespoon garlic, finely chopped

1 large onion, finely chopped

1 cup tomato purée

2 tablespoons chilli sauce

1 cup red or black kidney beans, soaked overnight and cooked till tender

Salt to taste

FOR EGGS

4 teaspoons vegetable oil

4 eggs

Salt to taste

White pepper powder to taste

TO SERVE

Toasted bread

Method

- For chilli beans, heat butter in a frying pan over medium heat. Add crushed nigella and fennel seeds with garlic and sauté till very fragrant.
- Add chopped onion, sauté till soft and stir in tomato purée with chilli sauce and bring the mixture to a simmer.
- Add the cooked beans with water in the resultant broth and add salt. Cook till the mixture thickens. Divide the beans among 4 serving plates or bowls.
- For the eggs, heat 1 teaspoon oil in a frying pan over medium heat. Gently break an egg into the pan and cook for 2 to 3 minutes till the white has set and yolk is just done. Sprinkle salt and pepper. Using a spatula, remove the fried egg and place it on top of the beans in the bowl. Repeat with the remaining eggs and beans.
- Serve hot with toasted bread.

Sun-dried Tamatar Ke Saath Bani Andey Ki Bhurji

सन–ड्राइड टमाटर के साथ बनी अंडे की भुर्जी

Scrambled Eggs With Sun-dried Tomatoes

Serves 4

Ingredients

4 eggs

¼ cup whole milk

1 tablespoon butter

1 teaspoon cumin seeds

2-inch piece ginger, finely grated

4 - 5 pieces sun-dried tomatoes, finely chopped

3 tablespoons parsley, finely chopped

Salt to taste

White pepper powder to taste

TO SERVE

8 slices of toast

Though many opt for the slightly chewy egg bhurji made with onions, tomatoes and green chillies, I prefer soft scrambled eggs mixed with the herby tang of sun-dried tomatoes. You could also experiment with roasted mushrooms, cheese and vinegared onions for a luxurious take on the old rumble-tumble.

Method

- Break eggs into a mixing bowl, add milk and whisk till frothy.
- Heat butter in a large frying pan over medium heat; add cumin seeds and ginger. When the cumin seeds begin to crackle, add the sun-dried tomatoes and parsley. Sauté for a minute.
- Remove pan from heat and gently pour in the egg mixture, stirring constantly. Add salt and pepper and return pan to heat. Cook, stirring continuously, till mixture begins to come together, but does not become lumpy.
- Remove from heat and serve immediately with hot toast.

Parsi Shaili Ke Andey

Parsi-style Egg Galette

Serves 4

Originally a French term describing flat round cakes or biscuits made by spreading batter on a griddle, here I use the word galette to describe the potato slices which remind me of galettes. A simple technique close to my heart, this was one of the first few things I learned at Le Cordon Bleu.

Ingredients

1 tablespoon butter
2 medium onions, finely chopped
2 green chillies, finely chopped
1 heaped teaspoon ginger-garlic paste
2 medium tomatoes, finely chopped
½ teaspoon turmeric powder
1 teaspoon kitchen king masala (See page 23 and NOTE*)
1 small green mango, finely chopped
½ cup finely chopped fresh coriander
3 medium potatoes, finely sliced and soaked in salted water for 20 minutes
Salt to taste
2 large eggs

Method

- Heat butter in a large frying pan over medium heat. Add onions and green chillies and sauté till the onions soften.
- Mix in ginger-garlic paste, tomatoes, turmeric and kitchen king masala and sauté till the tomatoes are pulpy and the mixture is very fragrant.
- Add green mango and coriander, and when coriander wilts, drain the potatoes and add to the pan with salt. Toss well to coat potatoes with the spices.
- Sprinkle 2 tablespoons water, cover and cook for about 4 to 5 minutes or till the potatoes are half done.
- Uncover the pan, sprinkle 1 tablespoon water and break the eggs onto the potatoes. Cover the pan and reduce heat to low. Cook for 5 to 7 minutes, or till the potatoes are done and the eggs have set completely.
- Serve hot with bread.

*NOTE: For a quick version of kitchen king masala, mix together 1 teaspoon each of cumin powder, coriander powder, turmeric powder, black pepper powder, 2 teaspoons red chilli powder and ½ teaspoon each of dried ginger powder, mustard powder, cinnamon powder, clove powder and ¼ teaspoon nutmeg powder.

Masaledar Cheese Soufflé

मसालेदार चीज़ सुफ़्ले

Spicy Cheese Soufflé

Serves 6

Ingredients

½ cup butter, chilled
6 eggs, separated
½ teaspoon red chilli powder
1 teaspoon white pepper powder
½ teaspoon dried ginger powder (sonth)
½ cup milk
3 tablespoons all-purpose flour (maida)
Salt to taste
½ cup finely grated cheese

I remember resolving to never make a soufflé again after having to make four varieties of it for my cookery examination. However, this turned out to be one of the many 'nevers' a student declares in his life. Cheese being my comfort food, I continued to turn out cheese soufflés using different cheeses. Once, I accidentally spilt a spice blend into the soufflé base and it resulted in a new direction of thought.

Method

- Grease a large soufflé mould or 6 small soufflé moulds liberally with butter and place in the freezer to chill.
- Preheat oven to 200°C/400°F/Gas 6.
- In a mixing bowl, combine the egg yolks with chilli powder, pepper powder, ginger powder, milk, flour and salt. Beat the mixture lightly.
- Add cheese and beat to mix thoroughly.
- Beat the egg whites till stiff and fold gently, but quickly into the cheese mixture in two batches.
- Remove the soufflé moulds from the freezer and fill three-fourth full with the prepared mixture. Place on the middle rack of the preheated oven and bake for 8 to 10 minutes till the soufflé has risen well and is golden all over.
- Remove from oven and serve immediately with salad.

SEAFOOD

The seas surrounding India and the many inland rivers abound with fish and seafood. Every region has its own special spice blends that complement the seafood available and enhance their flavour. But, the one common practice to all is the use of turmeric and salt (and sometimes chilli powder) in a pre-cooking rub that serves to disinfect the fish, as well as rid it of any unpleasant odours. The fish is then fried or cooked in curries. A dash of lime juice or vinegar firms up the delicate flesh and prevents it from disintegrating while cooking.

Seafood and spice are a match made in heaven. A light dusting of salt and pepper can do wonders to a fillet of fish or a handful of prawns; flavour-packed spice and herb blends transform already delicious fruits of the sea into gastronomic delights – think crabs sautéed in garlic butter, prawns drenched in Koliwada masala, crisp batter-fried Amritsari machchi and the pride of Bengal – shorshe ilish or hilsa in mustard sauce. And rice, appams (lacy pancakes made using fermented rice batter) and breads soaking up finger-licking seafood swimming in creamy, spiced coconut curries are the stuff of culinary dreams.

Kurlyanche Sukke

कुर्ल्यांचे सुक्के

Crab Pepper Fry

Serves 4

The first time I tasted this dish was in Mangaluru (Mangalore) where mud crabs were cooked in coconut oil. Here, I have used butter to give the dish the flavour of everyone's favourite butter pepper crab.

Ingredients

4 large crabs, each weighing approximately 500 gm
2 tablespoons butter
2 tablespoons tamarind pulp
1 teaspoon garlic paste
¼ teaspoon turmeric powder
2 tablespoons tomato purée
Salt to taste

FOR SPICE MIX

2 - 3 large dried red chillies
2 tablespoons coriander seeds
2 tablespoons black peppercorns
½ tablespoon cumin seeds
1 small sprig fresh curry leaves

FOR GARNISH

A few sprigs fresh coriander

Method

- To prepare the crabs, wash, clean and remove the outer top shell of the crabs and discard. Crack the claws and inner shell and drain the water. Combine the crab shells and claws with cold water in a saucepan and bring to a boil. Boil for about 3 to 4 minutes and drain away the water. Remove meat from shells.
- Heat butter in a large frying pan over medium heat; add tamarind pulp, garlic paste, turmeric and tomato purée and sauté for a minute. Add ground spice paste, stir to mix and cook till the mixture thickens.
- For spice mix, combine all ingredients in a frying pan and dry-roast over medium heat till very fragrant. Transfer the roasted spices to a mortar and pestle and crush to a slightly coarse powder.
- Add crab meat and claws with salt and mix well. Cook till the spice mixture coats the crabs well. Remove from heat, garnish with coriander and serve with rotis or parathas.

Kalwachi Kodi

कालवची कोडी

Oyster Curry

Serves 4

Oysters bring back memories of picnics at the seaside with Mum and Dad, when we would look for a patch of rocks from which we could pull out oysters. We would add them to leftover fish curry and enjoy it all over again—this time with a new flavour.

Ingredients

1 tablespoon vegetable oil

2 stalks fresh lemongrass

1-inch piece ginger, minced

6 cloves garlic, minced

2 large onions, finely chopped

2-inch piece fresh turmeric, finely chopped

1 cup tomato purée

1 tablespoon red chilli powder

1 tablespoon fish masala (See page 22)

1 cup fish stock or water

500 g shucked oysters

Salt to taste

Method

- Heat oil in a pan over medium heat. Crush the lemongrass using the back of a wooden spoon and add to the oil.
- Add ginger, garlic and onions, and sauté till the onions soften. Add chopped turmeric and sauté for a few seconds.
- Stir in tomato purée, red chilli powder and fish masala and cook, stirring constantly, till the oil rises to the surface.
- Add stock and bring the curry to a boil.
- Reduce heat, add oysters with salt and cook for 7 to 8 minutes till the oysters are done. Take care not to overcook the oysters as they will turn chewy.
- Serve hot with steamed rice or bread rolls.

"East Indian" Grilled Jhinge Laal Curry Mein

'ईस्ट इंडियन' ग्रिल्ड झींगे लाल करी में

Grilled Prawns In
East Indian Red Coastal Curry

Serves 4

"Are you a Bengali, then?" A question I'm often asked when I say I am East Indian. For those not in the know, this curry is not from Eastern India but from the East Indian community, the original inhabitants of Mumbai. The community was named for the British East India Company, which held sway in Bombay. The British are long gone, but the name has stayed on.

Ingredients

FOR PRAWNS

750 g prawns, shelled and deveined, with tails intact
Salt to taste
1 teaspoon white pepper powder
2 tablespoons vegetable oil
¼ cup roughly chopped fresh coriander

FOR SPICE PASTE

8 dried Kashmiri chillies
1 teaspoon turmeric powder
8 - 10 black peppercorns
½ teaspoon cumin seeds
½ teaspoon poppy seeds (khus khus)
½ teaspoon white sesame seeds (til)
4 cloves
1-inch cinnamon stick
1 tablespoon coriander seeds
1 cup freshly grated coconut

FOR CURRY

4 tablespoons vegetable oil
2 cups fish stock or water
Salt to taste
½ tablespoon black pepper powder
1 tablespoon brown palm vinegar

Method

- In a large mixing bowl, add the prawns with salt and pepper and mix well. Set aside for 5 minutes.
- Meanwhile, for spice paste, combine all ingredients in a mixer or processor jar with 3 or 4 tablespoons water and grind to a smooth paste.
- For curry, heat oil in a pan over low heat; add ground paste and fry, stirring constantly, till the oil rises to the surface.
- Stir in stock, salt and pepper and bring the curry to a boil. When the curry thickens, add vinegar, cook for a few seconds and remove from heat.
- Grease a grill or grill pan with oil and heat over medium-high flame. Spread the coriander evenly on a plate.
- Grill the marinated prawns for 2 minutes on each side till cooked through. Roll in the fresh coriander.
- Serve grilled prawns hot on a bed of curry with bread rolls or pão.

Masala Rawas

Indian Salmon Baked With Spices

Serves 4

मसाला रवास

Ingredients

- 2 tablespoons olive oil
- 1 tablespoon lime juice
- ½ teaspoon black pepper powder
- ½ teaspoon roasted cumin seeds, crushed
- 1 teaspoon red chilli powder
- ¼ teaspoon turmeric powder
- Salt to taste
- ½ tablespoon ginger-garlic paste
- 1 large (approx. 800 g) Indian salmon (rawas), cleaned and slit along the bone

This is a quick and simple dish to put together when in a hurry. Just apply spices to the fish, pop it in the oven and 10 minutes later—dinner's ready! Marinate the fish longer for a better flavour.

Method

- In a mixing bowl, combine olive oil with lime juice, pepper powder, crushed cumin, chilli powder, turmeric powder, salt and ginger-garlic paste. Whisk well.
- Place the fish on a platter and pour the prepared marinade and rub the fish with the mixture evenly. Cover and set aside for 15 minutes.
- Preheat oven to 180°C/350°F/Gas 4. Line a baking tray with foil and place the fish on it. Cover with another piece of foil and bake in the preheated oven for 10 to 15 minutes, or till the fish is cooked through.
- Serve hot with salad.

Paplet Ambotik

Sour And Spicy Pomfret Curry

Serves 4

The hot and sour combination of flavours is not restricted to Southeast Asian cuisine, but is also popular in coastal India, particularly Goa. This dish is reminiscent of many a childhood memory for most who live along the Indian coast. Here, kokum adds not just a sweetish sourness to the curry, but also a light blush.

पपलेट अंबोतिक

Ingredients

FOR MASALA PASTE

6 - 8 dried Kashmiri chillies, soaked in hot water for 1 hour

½ cup freshly grated coconut

8 - 10 cloves garlic, roughly chopped

1-inch piece ginger, roughly chopped

1 teaspoon cumin seeds

½ teaspoon turmeric powder

FOR CURRY

2 tablespoons vegetable oil

2 large pomfrets, sliced across the bone

2 cups fish stock or water

8 kokum rinds

Salt to taste

Method

- For masala paste, combine all ingredients in a mixer or processor jar with 2 to 3 tablespoons water and grind to a smooth paste.
- For curry, heat oil in a pan over low heat; add ground paste and cook, stirring constantly, till fragrant.
- Add the pomfret slices; cook for a minute and stir in the remaining ingredients. Bring the curry to a boil, reduce heat and simmer for about 5 minutes.
- Serve hot with steamed rice.

Kerala-style Machhli

केरला–स्टाइल मछली

Riverboat Fish

Serves 4

Though my style of cooking is influenced strongly by French cuisine, I am besotted with regional Indian cuisine. The flavours, textures and colours of a simple moileé (coconut-based sauce or curry) from Kerala inspired this dish, and the French influence comes through in the technique of grilling the fish.

Ingredients

FOR FISH
4 X 200 g sole fillets
Salt to taste
Juice of 1 lemon
1 tablespoon melted butter
1 tablespoon coconut oil

FOR COCONUT SAUCE
2 teaspoons coconut oil
1 teaspoon black mustard seeds
1 sprig fresh curry leaves
2 - 3 dried red chillies, broken into pieces
1 teaspoon turmeric powder
1 large onion, pureed
1 cup fish stock
1 cup coconut milk
Salt to taste
Juice of 1 lime

FOR GARNISH
A few sprigs fresh coriander
2 tablespoons fresh coconut gratings

Method

- Smear the fish fillets over with salt and lemon juice, toss lightly and set aside.
- For coconut sauce, heat coconut oil in a pan over medium heat and add mustard seeds, curry leaves and red chillies.
- When the spices crackle, add turmeric and onion. Sauté for a few seconds or till the onion is cooked.
- Add fish stock and coconut milk and bring the sauce to a boil, stirring constantly. Simmer till the sauce thickens. Remove from heat and add salt and lime juice.
- To cook the fish, heat butter and oil in a grill pan over medium heat; place the marinated fish in the pan and sear on both sides for a few seconds. Reduce heat to low, cover and cook for 3 to 4 minutes or till the fish is just tender.
- Drizzle coconut sauce liberally over the grilled fish.
- Garnish with coriander and coconut gratings. Serve hot with rice.

POULTRY

There was a time when chicken was reserved for special occasions. Today, with the poultry industry in overdrive, chicken is more popular than any other meat and is a ubiquitous dish on restaurant and home menus. Roasted, fried, stir-fried, curried, baked or steamed, chicken lends itself to every Indian regional cooking style and method. Searingly hot and spicy chicken 65, velvety butter chicken, stir-fried in chatpata Indo-Chinese sauces, smeared in roasted coconut and spices in a shagoti, or enrobed in a rich rezala, chicken rules our culinary roosts.

Achaari Beer Murgh

Chicken With Pickling Spices And Beer

अचारी बियर मुर्ग

Serves 4 - 6

This recipe brings back memories of college, when part of cleaning up after a celebration included making an after-party dish with the leftover beer and chicken, and flavouring it with pickle to add more zing.

Ingredients

FOR CHICKEN

1½ cups lager beer

2 heaped tablespoons pickle masala (See page 25)

Salt to taste

Juice of 1 large lime

4 tablespoons melted butter

1 kg whole chicken with skin

FOR SALAD

8 - 10 cherry tomatoes

1 large onion, cut into rings

1 small head iceberg lettuce, torn into large pieces

2 teaspoons balsamic vinegar

Salt to taste

Black pepper powder to taste

1-inch piece ginger, finely grated

Method

- For chicken, in a large mixing bowl, whisk beer with pickle masala, salt, lime juice and 3 tablespoons butter. Set aside for 10 minutes and allow the flavours to merge.
- Place the chicken in a bowl and rub the prepared beer marinade evenly. Cover and set aside for 2 hours, turning the chicken over at regular intervals.
- Preheat oven to 220°C/425°F/Gas 7.
- Place the marinated chicken on a large baking tray lined with foil. Pour the leftover marinade in a small ovenproof bowl and place inside the chicken cavity.
- Roast the chicken in the preheated oven for 30 minutes. Brush with the remaining butter, cover with foil and roast for another 30 minutes, or till the chicken is tender and juicy.
- For salad, toss all the ingredients together in a mixing bowl.
- Serve the chicken hot with salad.

Murgh Bharwan Mirch

Chicken-stuffed Chillies

Serves 3 - 4

This recipe is what I call my inside-out version of a spicy chicken curry I once ate in Rajasthan. I substituted the numerous chillies in the spicy curry with large Jodhpur chillies (commonly known as Athana {pickle} chillies; they are large, broad and fleshy with a mild spiciness to them), and stuffed them with the chicken. And voilà! The curry itself became a sauce!

Ingredients

FOR CHICKEN

1 tablespoon mustard oil
½ teaspoon asafoetida powder (hing)
1 teaspoon mustard seeds
1 tablespoon garlic paste
300 g minced chicken
1 teaspoon garam masala (See page 20)
Salt to taste
6 - 8 medium Jodhpur chillies, slit open along one side and deseeded

FOR SAUCE

1 teaspoon vegetable oil
½ teaspoon carom seeds (ajwain)
1 cup tomato purée
½ teaspoon paprika
A pinch cinnamon powder
½ cup yoghurt, whisked
¼ cup grated cheese
Salt to taste
White pepper powder to taste

Method

- For chicken, heat mustard oil in a frying pan over medium heat till smoking. Add asafoetida powder and mustard seeds.
- When the spices crackle, add garlic paste and sauté till fragrant. Add chicken mince, garam masala and salt. Cook till the mince is done and the mixture is dry. Remove from heat and cool slightly.
- Using a spoon, stuff the mince mixture into the chillies.
- Preheat oven to 150°C/300°F/Gas 2. Place the stuffed chillies on a baking tray lined with foil, cover with another piece of foil and bake in the oven for 7 to 8 minutes, or till the chillies are tender. Remove from the oven.
- For sauce, heat oil in a frying pan over medium heat and add carom seeds. When they begin to crackle, add tomato purée, paprika and cinnamon and cook till the purée is thick, glossy and fragrant.
- Whisk in yoghurt, cheese, salt and pepper and bring the sauce to a simmer, stirring constantly.
- Arrange the stuffed chillies on a serving plate and serve the sauce on the side. Serve with any bread of your choice.

"Anglo-Indian" Shaili Mein Bana Murgh

Chicken Country Captain

Serves 4

This is a favourite Anglo Indian recipe believed to have been created by the British during the Raj. This version has been enriched with pistachios, cashews and cream, giving it a new elegance.

Ingredients

FOR SPICE PASTE

½ cup grated fresh coconut

½ cup broken cashew nuts

½ cup pistachios

7 pods green cardamom

7 cloves

1 teaspoon poppy seeds (khus khus), lightly roasted

1 teaspoon cumin seeds

1½ tablespoons red chilli powder

1 teaspoon garam masala (See page 20)

FOR CHICKEN

6 tablespoons clarified butter (ghee)

2 large bay leaves

2 medium onions, finely sliced

1 tablespoon garlic paste

1 teaspoon ginger paste

1 kg chicken, cut into large pieces

2½ cups chicken stock

½ cup yoghurt, whisked well

⅓ cup heavy cream

Salt to taste

Black pepper powder to taste

Method

- For spice paste, combine all the ingredients in a blender or food processor and grind to a smooth paste.
- For chicken, heat half the clarified butter in a large frying pan; add bay leaves with onions and sauté till onions soften.
- Add garlic paste, ginger paste and chicken, and sauté till the chicken is evenly browned.
- Heat the remaining clarified butter in another large pan over medium heat. Add ground spice paste and sauté till very fragrant, sprinkle with some stock if required, to prevent the paste from burning.
- Add chicken with onions and mix well. Cook for a minute, then stir in the stock with remaining ingredients. Cook till the sauce is thick and glossy and has evenly coated the chicken.
- Serve hot with bread or rice.

Murgh Dhansak

मुर्ग धनसक

Chicken Dhansak

Serves 4

I have enjoyed the famous Parsi dhansak and its numerous variations made by my Parsi friends. And though they do an unparalleled job, I couldn't resist making a version of my own. Here, I have broiled the chicken (by applying heat only from above) to give it an interesting texture.

Ingredients

FOR CHICKEN
4 chicken breasts
1 teaspoon ginger paste
1 teaspoon garlic paste
½ teaspoon red chilli powder
Juice of 1 lime
2 tablespoons clarified butter (ghee)

FOR DHANSAK
1 cup mixed lentils, washed and soaked for 1 hour
1 cup diced pumpkin (kaddu)
2 cups fresh fenugreek leaves (methi), washed well
3 cups water
1 tablespoon vegetable oil
1 tablespoon clarified butter (ghee)
1 tablespoon ginger-garlic paste
1 large onion, ground to a paste
2 medium tomatoes, puréed
2 tablespoons dhansak masala (See page 24)
Salt to taste
Black pepper powder

Method

- For chicken, make gashes in the chicken breasts and place in a mixing bowl. Add ginger paste, garlic paste, chilli powder, lime juice and clarified butter. Mix well, cover and set aside for 1 hour.
- For dhansak, combine lentils, pumpkin and fenugreek leaves in a pressure cooker. Add 3 cups water and cook till the pressure is released 4 times (4 whistles). Remove from heat and allow the pressure to settle.
- Pass the cooked lentil-pumpkin mixture through a strainer to get a smooth purée. Discard any fibrous leftover fenugreek stems.
- Heat oil and clarified butter in a large saucepan, kadhai or wok over medium heat. Add ginger-garlic paste and sauté till the mixture is very fragrant.
- Add onion paste, tomato purée and dhansak masala and cook, stirring continuously, till the mixture is fragrant and the oil rises to the surface.
- Add the lentil-pumpkin purée, salt and pepper and bring the mixture to a simmer.
- Set oven to a broiler/grill setting and preheat to 180°C/350°F/Gas 4.
- Place the marinated chicken on a baking tray lined with foil and broil in the oven for 10 to 15 minutes or till tender. Remove from oven and cut into long slices.
- Ladle the dhansak into serving bowls and place the broiled chicken on top. Serve with bread rolls.

Nimboo Achaari Murgh

Lemon Chicken

Serves 4

नींबू अचारी मुर्ग

Uncle Trevor Pierce with his fancy hats was an Anglo Indian neighbour who will always be remembered in our wadi. He would dry lemons on the terrace and then pickle them— awesome stuff—a cousin of preserved lemons! Preserved lemons have long been used as a condiment in Moroccan cuisine. They make for a refreshing marinade in this chicken curry.

Ingredients

FOR CHICKEN

2 boneless chicken breasts

1 large preserved lemon, roughly chopped (recipe below)

½ teaspoon black pepper powder

½ teaspoon red chilli powder

1 teaspoon cumin powder

Salt to taste

Oil for basting

FOR SALAD

2 teaspoons olive oil

8 - 10 cherry tomatoes

2 red capsicums, cut into strips

1 large green capsicum, cut into strips

1 small head romaine lettuce

1 preserved lemon, cut into quarters

½ teaspoon black pepper powder

1 teaspoon honey

Method

- For chicken, place the chicken breast pieces on a plate and add chopped preserved lemon, pepper powder, chilli powder, cumin powder and salt. Rub the chicken with the spices and set aside to marinate for 15 to 20 minutes.
- For salad, combine all the ingredients and toss well. Set aside for 5 minutes.
- Heat a grill pan over medium-high heat and grill the chicken, turning regularly and basting with oil for 4 to 5 minutes, or till tender. Place salad ingredients around chicken and grill till light char marks appear on the vegetables.
- Serve the grilled lemon chicken hot with salad.

NOTE: Though preserved lemons are available at gourmet or specialty stores, it's easy and fun to make some for yourself. Wash and wipe dry 6 lemons and slit them crosswise. Fill about a fistful of coarse salt or sea salt into a clean, dry glass jar and add the lemons to it, packing them in with salt. When 3 lemons are added, push in 2 to 3 sprigs rosemary and a cinnamon stick. Add the remaining lemons with some more salt and ¼ cup lemon juice. Close the jar and keep in a well-lit place for 3 days, shaking the jar once every day. The lemons can be refrigerated and stored for up to 6 months.

MEATS

Spices have played a major role in cooking meats in India. The preservative qualities of spices have helped to prevent spoilage and given the meat an almost pickled flavour. The combination of spices used to cook meats depends on regional and cultural preferences. Thus Kashmiri Pandits cook their meats in thin, lightly spiced, aromatic gravies; the Rajputs of Rajasthan roast meats in heavy-duty whole spices, while in the Northeast the principle is minimum spice with maximum flavour. Mustard oil made from the tiny black seeds that pack a powerful punch, is the cooking medium of choice in Punjab and Bengal, while in the south, sesame oil lends its nutty flavour to round off a dish. And everywhere, there are chillies of all colours, shapes and sizes to raise the heat as in Goan vindalho and Bengali kosha mangsho (spicy lamb/beef or mutton curry).

Kodava Yerchi Kari

Coorgi-style Lamb Shank Stew

Serves 4

कोडावा एरची करी

The Kodava community in Karnataka is known for its meat delicacies. A fierce tribe, the Kodavas cling to their culinary heritage in a very special way. Here's my adaptation of one of their well-known dishes.

Ingredients

FOR SPICE MIX

6 - 8 shallots, peeled and roughly chopped

1 tablespoon garam masala (See page 20)

½ teaspoon turmeric powder

4 cloves

2 teaspoons poppy seeds (khus khus)

1-inch cinnamon stick

2 pods green cardamom

2 - 3 fish tamarind rinds (kadampuli) or kokum rinds

3 tablespoons vegetable oil

FOR LAMB

4 small lamb shanks

Salt to taste

2 cups vegetable stock

FOR GARNISH

A few sprigs fresh coriander, roughly chopped

Method

- For spice mix, in a mixer or processor jar, combine shallots with garam masala, turmeric powder, cloves, poppy seeds, cinnamon, cardamom, kadampuli and 1 tablespoon oil. Grind to a smooth paste.
- For lamb/beef, transfer the paste to a large plate, add lamb/beef shanks and rub the paste evenly. Sprinkle over with salt and rub well again. Cover and leave to marinate for one hour.
- Preheat oven to 200˚C/400°F/Gas 6.
- Heat oil in a large frying pan over medium heat; add the marinated meat and sear evenly on all sides. Transfer the meat to a deep baking tray lined with foil. Pour 1 cup stock over the meat and cover with another piece of foil.
- Place tray in the preheated oven and cook for 1 hour. Halfway through cooking, pour the remaining stock over. Cover again and cook till the lamb/beef is tender.
- Remove from the oven, garnish with coriander and serve hot with rice.

Lucknavi Chaamp

Lucknow-style Lamb Chops

Serves 4

लखनवी चाँप

Ingredients

8 lamb chops
1 tablespoon meat masala (See page 21)
2 tablespoons almond paste
1 tablespoon milk masala (See page 25)
1 tablespoon ginger-garlic paste
Salt to taste
¼ cup whole milk
Clarified butter (ghee) for shallow-frying

One of my most enjoyable meals was on a wintry evening in Lucknow, when we chanced upon a vendor selling chaamp (or mutton chops), cooked over coal. I enjoyed the smoky flavour of the meat mingled with the rich fragrance of saffron. In this recipe, the milk masala recreates those flavours perfectly.

Method

- In a large mixing bowl, combine lamb/beef chops with meat masala, almond paste, milk masala, ginger-garlic paste, salt and milk. Cover and set aside for 20 minutes.
- Heat clarified butter in a heavy-bottomed pan over low heat; add the marinated chops with the remaining marinade. Cover and cook till the lamb/beef is tender and done.
- Serve hot with sheermal rotis or with salad as a starter.

Pahadi Gosht

Himalayan Mutton Curry

Serves 4

Ingredients

2 tablespoons clarified butter (ghee)
2 large onions, finely sliced
500 g mutton on the bone, cut into 2-inch pieces
Salt to taste
1 teaspoon red chilli powder
1 cup fresh tomato purée
1 heaped tablespoon meat masala (See page 21)
4 cups mutton stock, plus more if required

I first ate this dish in the lap of the Himalayas on a cold, wet monsoon day. The warmth of the spices and the unique flavour of the local meat were unforgettable. I often cook the dish in a pressure cooker as I believe it makes the flavours even more intense.

Method

- Heat clarified butter in a deep, heavy-bottomed pan over medium heat. Add onions, mutton and salt. Cook, stirring and turning the mutton constantly, till all the moisture dries up and onions begin to brown.
- Add chilli powder and tomato purée and cook for 2 to 3 minutes.
- Add meat masala and cook, stirring continuously, till the clarified butter floats on the surface.
- Stir in stock and more salt if required. Cover the pan and place a heavy object on the lid to seal the pan. Cook for 1 hour, stirring the mutton once or twice in between, adding more stock if required.
- Serve hot with rotis.

Lonvas

East Indian Lamb And Ash Gourd Curry

Serves 4

The very idea of cooking meats with vegetables is to make an all-in-one dish, which is not only flavourful, but nutritious as well, making for a great mini meal. The original dish uses pumpkin, but I also like this version using ash gourd.

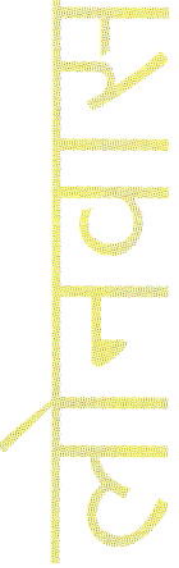

Ingredients

500 g lamb on the bone, cut into 2-inch cubes

3 cups mutton stock

Salt to taste

1-inch piece ginger, crushed

4 tablespoons clarified butter (ghee)

8 cloves garlic, finely sliced

2 tablespoons meat masala (See page 21)

1 cup diced ash gourd (petha)

1 teaspoon black pepper powder

½ cup thick coconut milk

2 tablespoons tamarind pulp

Method

- Combine the lamb/beef with stock, salt and ginger in a pan and bring to a boil over medium-high heat. Cook the lamb/beef till tender, skimming off and discarding any scum that rises to the surface, at regular intervals. Strain the lamb/beef, reserving the stock.
- Heat clarified butter in a large frying pan over medium heat; add garlic and sauté till golden and crisp. Add meat masala with 2 tablespoons stock and sauté till very fragrant.
- Add ash gourd with cooked meat, pepper and more salt if required. Fry for a minute.
- Stir in coconut milk, tamarind pulp and reserved stock and bring to a boil, stirring constantly. Simmer for 10 to 15 minutes or till the ash gourd is cooked.
- Serve hot with rice.

Saag Gosht

Lamb Chops With Sautéed Spinach

Serves 4

I had always wondered why saag gosht should have such rich, thick gravy submerging the flavours of the meat. Why not keep the goodness of spinach intact by leaving it light and salad-like? Here, I have done just that!

Ingredients

FOR LAMB CHOPS

8 lamb chops, washed and excess fat trimmed
1 tablespoon meat masala (See page 21)
1 tablespoon ginger paste
1 tablespoon garlic paste
Salt to taste
2 tablespoons mustard oil
1½ cups vegetable stock

FOR SPINACH

1 tablespoon mustard oil
2 dried Kashmiri chillies, broken into pieces
2 large onions, finely chopped
1 teaspoon coriander powder
1 teaspoon cumin powder
½ teaspoon black pepper powder
750 g spinach, washed, pat-dried and roughly chopped
Salt to taste

FOR SERVING

Lemon wedges

Method

- In a large mixing bowl, combine the lamb/beef chops with meat masala, ginger paste, garlic paste and salt. Cover and leave to marinate for 1 hour.
- Heat oil in a frying pan over medium heat; add the marinated lamb/beef chops with the remaining marinade and sear evenly on all sides. Stir in stock, reduce heat to low and cook, stirring occasionally, till the meat is tender.
- For spinach, heat oil in a frying pan over medium heat and add chillies.
- When chillies sizzle, add onions and sauté for a few seconds till fragrant. Add coriander powder, cumin powder and pepper powder and sauté for a minute.
- Add spinach and salt, toss well and remove from heat just as it begins to wilt. Do not overcook.
- Arrange the lamb/beef chops on a bed of spiced spinach with lemon wedges on the side. Serve hot with bread rolls and salad.

VEGETABLES AND LENTILS

India is home to a plethora of vegetables, legumes and pulses. There is no dearth of options for vegetarians who form a large part of the Indian population. Lightly sautéed with a smattering of spices, heavily doused in rich curries, steamed or grilled, local vegetables always have pride of place on an Indian table. Foogath, chorchori, saag, patal bhaji, thoran, upkari, shaak – an Indian vegetable dish by any name, from any region, tells of the symbiotic relationship between the produce of the land and the spices that perfume it.

Legumes and lentils are rich sources of protein for those who opt for a vegetarian way of life. Dal, sambhar, rasam, ussal, chana, chhole, amti, varan – earthy legumes are brought to life with a baptism of sizzling spices. Garlic, turmeric, cumin, mustard seeds and asafoetida have a natural affinity for legumes and pulses, their innate properties counteracting any adverse effects of the beans.

Chhole Anardana

Curried Chickpeas With Pomegranate

छोले अनारदाना

Serves 4

I hate chhole! That's what I used to think until I sampled some in Punjab. One spoonful of the dish at a dhaba there changed my perception forever! Served with farm-fresh carrots and cucumbers, and sizzling hot bhature (leavened fried bread), I fell in love with the dish. Here, I've tried substituting dried pomegranate with fresh. The result is a surprisingly sweet and sour tang that makes this version even more unique.

Ingredients

1 cup chickpeas (kabuli chana), soaked overnight with a pinch of sodium bicarbonate
1-inch cinnamon stick
1 pod black cardamom
1½ teaspoons cumin seeds
4 cups water
1 tablespoon vegetable oil
½ tablespoon ginger-garlic paste
1 large onion, puréed
1 heaped teaspoon chhole masala (See page 18)
2 cups tomato purée
Salt to taste
½ cup fresh pomegranate kernels
¼ cup fresh mint leaves

Method

- Drain the chickpeas and rinse well. Combine the chickpeas with cinnamon, black cardamom, ½ teaspoon cumin seeds and 4 cups water in a pressure cooker. Place over medium heat and cook till pressure is released 4 to 5 times (4 - 5 whistles). Remove from heat and allow pressure to settle.
- Heat oil in a large frying pan over medium heat and add the remaining 1 teaspoon cumin seeds. When they crackle, add ginger-garlic paste, onion purée and chhole masala and cook till the mixture is fragrant.
- Add tomato purée and cook till oil floats on the surface.
- Add salt with cooked chickpeas and cook till the mixture thickens.
- Remove from heat and mix in pomegranate kernels and mint.
- Serve hot with puris or parathas.

Jeerawale Khumb

Cumin-scented Mushrooms

Serves 2 - 3

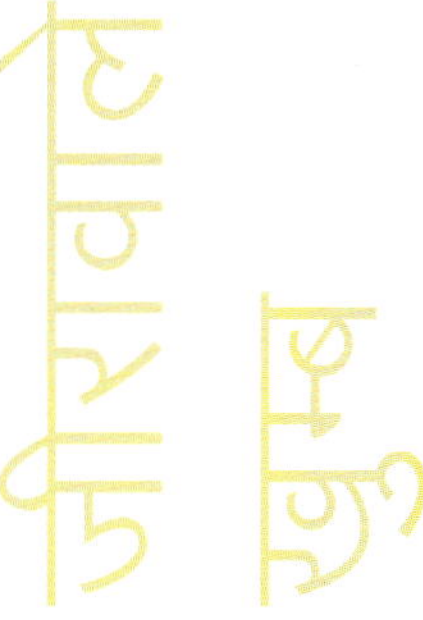

Ingredients

2 teaspoons vegetable oil
1 teaspoon cumin seeds
2 dried red chillies, broken into pieces
4 cloves garlic, finely chopped
1 large green capsicum, finely chopped
1 large onion, sliced into rings
¾ teaspoon turmeric powder
300 g button mushrooms, quartered
Salt to taste

Sometimes, a single ingredient can bring out the essence of a vegetable better than a spice blend. This is a quick recipe and perfect for times when unexpected guests drop by for a meal.

Method

- Heat oil in a frying pan over medium heat and add cumin seeds. When they crackle, add red chillies and garlic and sauté till fragrant.
- Add capsicum, onion rings and turmeric and sauté till the onion softens.
- Add mushrooms and salt and toss well. Cook till the mushrooms are heated through and slightly tender.
- Serve hot with bread, rotis or parathas.

Paneer Tulsi Makhani

Grilled Spiced Paneer With Buttery Tomato And Basil Gravy

पनीर तुलसी मखानी

Serves 4

Flavoured cheesecakes inspired me to make spiced paneer. After all, if cream cheese could be flavoured with fruit, why couldn't cottage cheese be flavoured with spices? And, the tulsi in the makhani? Well, that was just the result of boredom—eating the same kind of makhani!

Ingredients

FOR SPICED PANEER

2 litres whole milk
1 teaspoon turmeric powder
1 teaspoon white pepper powder
1 teaspoon salt
1½ tablespoons vinegar or lime juice
2 tablespoons vegetable oil

FOR MAKHANI GRAVY

6 large tomatoes, quartered
½ cup tomato purée
1 large onion, sliced
4 cloves garlic
1-inch piece ginger, sliced
1 teaspoon Kashmiri chilli powder
2 tablespoons butter
Salt to taste
7 - 8 holy basil leaves (tulsi), plus to garnish

Method

- For spiced paneer, combine milk with turmeric, white pepper and salt in a saucepan and bring to a boil over medium-high heat. When the milk boils, add vinegar or lemon juice and allow the milk to curdle completely.
- Strain the curdled milk through a cheesecloth placed over a strainer and tie into a tight bundle. The whey can be reserved and used as a stock in soups and lentil dishes.
- Plunge the bundle in iced water for a few minutes. Remove and squeeze out extra water. Place the bundle on a chopping board and weigh down with a saucepan for 10 to 15 minutes till the paneer is firm and holds its shape.
- Cut the paneer into rectangular slices of even thickness. Set aside.
- For makhani gravy, combine tomatoes with tomato purée, onion, garlic, ginger and chilli powder in a saucepan with 2 cups water and cook over medium heat till the mixture is pulpy. Transfer to a blender and blend to a slightly chunky purée.
- Heat butter in a frying pan and add the purée. Add salt and basil leaves and cook till the gravy thickens.
- To grill the paneer, brush a grill pan liberally with oil and heat over medium-high heat. Place the paneer pieces on it and grill, turning at regular intervals, till grill marks appear.
- Place the grilled spiced paneer on a bed of tulsi makhani gravy, garnish with tulsi leaves and serve hot with any bread of your choice.

Bhein Kofte Ki Kadhi

भें कोफ्ते की कढ़ी

Lotus Root Dumplings In Yoghurt Curry

Serves 4

The only form in which I had ever sampled lotus root was in a yakhni (fortified stock or broth supped as a soup, and also used as a base for making pilafs and biryanis). I loved the combination of earthy, almost sweet lotus root, with tangy yoghurt, and wondered if it would work without the fennel and dried ginger. So I tried the Bengali 5-spice (paanch phoran) instead and walked away quite pleased with the outcome.

Ingredients

FOR KOFTE

400 g lotus root (bhein), peeled and boiled till tender
½ teaspoon coriander powder
½ teaspoon cumin powder
1 teaspoon garam masala (See page 20)
Salt to taste
Oil for shallow-frying

FOR CURRY

2 cups yoghurt, whisked
2 tablespoons gram flour (besan)
½ teaspoon turmeric powder
2 green chillies, crushed
1-inch piece ginger, crushed
1 teaspoon vegetable oil
¼ teaspoon fenugreek seeds (methi dana)
½ teaspoon cumin seeds
½ teaspoon black mustard seeds
½ teaspoon nigella seeds (kalonji)
½ teaspoon fennel seeds (saunf)
Salt to taste
3 - 4 sprigs fresh parsley, finely chopped

Method

- For kofte, grate the boiled lotus root and mash well. Add coriander powder, cumin powder, garam masala and salt. Mix well.
- Divide the mixture into large lime-sized portions and shape each portion into a round dumpling.
- Heat oil on a griddle over medium heat and shallow-fry the dumplings, turning regularly, till golden and crisp. Remove and drain on absorbent paper.
- For curry, in a saucepan, whisk yoghurt with gram flour, crushed chillies, ginger and 1 cup water. Place pan on medium heat and bring curry to a boil, stirring constantly.
- Heat vegetable oil in a small pan over medium heat and add fenugreek, cumin, mustard, nigella and fennel seeds. As soon as the spices crackle, add them to the boiling curry with salt. Reduce heat to low and simmer for 1 minute. Add parsley and remove from heat.
- Add the kofte to the curry and serve hot with rice.

Raswali Masala Karari Bhindi

Crispy Okra In Spiced Tomato Curry

Serves 4

Young, tender okra (ladies' fingers) not only have great flavour, but lend themselves very well to being fried crisp. This tangy, crispy okra makes any curry taste even better!

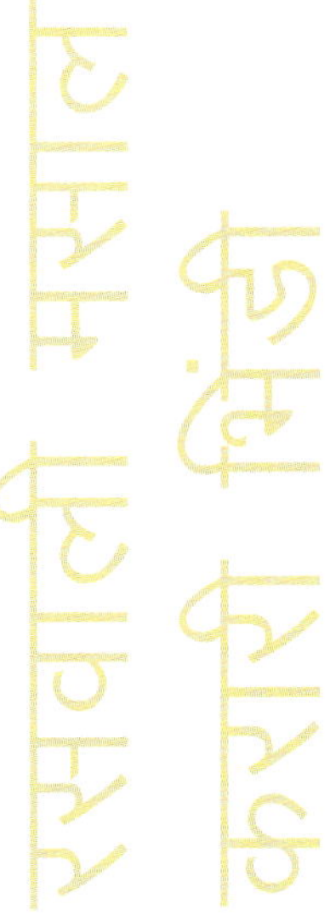

Ingredients

FOR OKRA

600 g okra (bhindi), tops and tips cut off and sliced lengthwise
1 teaspoon salt
1 tablespoon rice flour
1 teaspoon red chilli powder
¼ teaspoon asafoetida powder (hing)
Oil for deep-frying
½ teaspoon dried mango powder (amchur)

FOR GRAVY

1 tablespoon vegetable oil
1-inch cinnamon stick
2 pods green cardamom
1 medium onion, finely chopped
1 heaped teaspoon ginger-garlic paste
4 large tomatoes, puréed
1 teaspoon red chilli powder
¼ teaspoon fenugreek seeds (methi dana), roasted and powdered
½ teaspoon coriander powder
½ teaspoon cumin powder
A pinch of sugar
Salt to taste

Method

- Place the sliced okra on a large plate and sprinkle over with salt. Toss well and set aside for 10 minutes. The salt will make the okra release quite a bit of moisture.
- Drain the okra and pat dry with a clean dry kitchen towel. Transfer to a fresh plate, add rice flour, chilli powder and asafoetida. Mix well.
- For gravy, heat oil in a frying pan over medium heat and add cinnamon and cardamom. When the spices sizzle, add onion and ginger-garlic paste; sauté till the onion is translucent.
- Stir in puréed tomatoes with powdered spices and sugar. Cook till the gravy is thick and glossy. Mix in salt and remove from heat.
- Heat oil in a kadhai over medium heat and deep-fry okra till crisp and golden. Remove and drain on absorbent kitchen paper. While the fried okra is still hot, sprinkle over with dried mango powder and toss well.
- Ladle the gravy into a bowl and sprinkle over liberally with the crisp spiced okra. Serve with rotis.

Kalonjiwali Shatavari

कालोंजीवली शतवारी

Nigella-scented Asparagus

Serves 4

Ingredients

4 - 5 cups water

500 g tender asparagus (shatavari) spears

1 tablespoon vegetable oil

2 teaspoons nigella seeds (kalonji)

2 teaspoons white sesame seeds (til)

½ teaspoon white pepper powder

Salt to taste

Nigella seeds have an earthy-cum-nutty flavour, which goes well with tender, young asparagus spears.

Method

- Bring 4 to 5 cups water to a rapid boil in a large pan over high heat. Add asparagus spears and turn off the burner. Allow the asparagus to blanch for 30 to 40 seconds; drain the water and place the asparagus in a large bowl of iced water. Set aside for a minute and drain. Pat the asparagus dry.
- Heat oil in a large frying pan over medium heat; add nigella seeds and sesame seeds. When the spices crackle and sesame seeds turn golden, add white pepper powder with blanched asparagus and salt.
- Toss well and cook till the asparagus is heated through. Cook for a minute and remove from heat.
- Serve as a warm salad or side dish.

Sabut Urad Ki Dal

साबुत उड़द की दाल

White Lentils Stewed In Milk With Spices

Serves 4

Ingredients

1½ cups split white lentils (urad dal), washed and soaked for 1 hour
3 cups skimmed milk
1 tablespoon mustard oil
1 teaspoon cumin seeds
1 large fresh red chilli, slit
2-inch piece ginger, cut into fine strips
½ teaspoon turmeric powder
1 teaspoon red chilli powder
Salt to taste
A few sprigs fresh coriander, finely chopped

I first encountered this dish at the table of an old Delhi family. This was the first time I saw lentils cooked in this way. I had never really liked lentils until I sampled this dish, which gave me a whole new perception of the humble staple.

Method

- Drain the lentils and combine with milk in a saucepan. Place over medium heat and cook, stirring at regular intervals, till tender but not mushy. When done, remove from heat and fluff with a fork.
- Heat oil in a large frying pan over medium heat. Add cumin seeds, red chilli and ginger.
- When the cumin seeds crackle, add turmeric powder, chilli powder, cooked lentils and salt. Stir well. Cover and cook for 2 minutes.
- Remove from heat, sprinkle over with fresh coriander and serve hot.

SPICES
FINE ART
EMPORIUM
Crafters
FOREX
SPICE

BREADS AND CEREALS

Traditional Indian breads are unleavened flatbreads cooked on a hot griddle (tava) or on hot coals. There are also leavened breads cooked in a tandoor, or today, in ovens. In addition, there are steamed rice breads, puffed up deep-fried globes, lacy rice flour pancakes and the Portuguese pão and British sandwich loaf. The adventurous Indian palate and the abundance of spices close at hand have created an unrivalled array of flavoursome breads to accompany any meal.

And with cereals, the romance with spices continues. Rice, biryanis, pulaos and other cereal dishes take on a new personality when the spices come calling. A sprinkling of spices or herbs and humdrum semolina, barley, sorghum, oats and millets begin to exude a tantalising aroma that captivates the taste buds.

Chhole Aur Jau Ka Pulao

छोले और जौं का पुलाओ

Chickpea And Barley Pilaf

Serves 4

The chewy texture of nutritious barley makes a delicious contrast to soft, spicy chickpeas.

Ingredients

1½ cups pearl barley (jau)
4 cups vegetable stock
Salt to taste
1 tablespoon vegetable oil
2-inch piece ginger, finely chopped
4 cloves garlic, finely chopped
2 teaspoons red chilli flakes
2 heaped teaspoons chhole masala (See page 18)
1 cup cooked chickpeas (kabuli chana)
A few sprigs fresh parsley, finely chopped
Juice of 1 lime

Method

- Combine barley with vegetable stock and salt in a saucepan. Cook over medium-high heat, adding more water if necessary, till tender. Drain away any extra liquid.
- Heat oil in a large pan over medium heat; add ginger and garlic and sauté till the ginger softens and the garlic turns golden.
- Add chilli flakes, chhole masala and chickpeas and stir well. Add barley with parsley and mix well.
- Add salt if required, remove from heat and squeeze in lime juice.
- Serve hot with raita.

Kadhi Patta Thepla

कढ़ी पत्ता थेपला

Pan-fried Flatbreads Flavoured With Curry Leaves

Makes 8 - 10 theplas

Ingredients

- 2 cups wholewheat flour (atta), plus extra for dusting
- 1 teaspoon red chilli powder
- 1 teaspoon turmeric powder
- 2 sprigs fresh curry leaves, shredded
- ½ teaspoon carom seeds (ajwain)
- Salt to taste
- ½ teaspoon sugar
- ½ cup sour yoghurt, whisked
- Vegetable oil for shallow-frying

The highlight of any picnic or train journey for my Gujarati friends is feasting on bitter-sweet, salty, spicy theplas. The spicy flatbreads are usually made with fenugreek leaves, but here, I have used curry leaves to add some zing.

Method

- In a large mixing bowl, combine flour, chilli powder, turmeric, curry leaves, carom seeds, salt and sugar.
- Add yoghurt and mix well. Knead in just enough water to make a smooth, soft dough.
- Knead in 1 tablespoon oil; cover the dough with a damp cheesecloth and leave it to rest for 10 to 15 minutes.
- Divide the dough into lime-sized portions. Roll out each portion into a thin round 5-inch disc, about ¼ inch thick, dusting lightly with flour as you roll.
- Heat a griddle or tawa over medium heat and place a rolled disc (thepla) on it. Cook for 2 to 3 seconds and flip the thepla over. Drizzle ½ teaspoon oil around the edges and cook, pressing down with a spatula for a few seconds. Flip over again, drizzle oil and cook for a few more seconds till brown spots appear on both sides and the thepla is fragrant. Remove to a plate. Repeat with the remaining theplas.
- Serve hot with yoghurt or pickle.

Dhania, Saunf, Ajwain Aur Kalonji Naan

धनिया, सौंफ, अजवाइन और कलौंजी नान

Coriander, Fennel, Carom And Nigella Flatbreads

Makes 8 - 10 naans

Well, the name says it all! So many flavours added to this already delicious bread make it even more delectable. And you can eat it as a snack too!

Ingredients

FOR SPICE MIXTURE

1½ tablespoons coriander seeds

1½ tablespoons fennel seeds (saunf)

1 tablespoon carom seeds (ajwain)

1 tablespoon nigella seeds (kalonji)

FOR NAAN

2 teaspoons dry yeast granules

1 teaspoon sugar

1 cup warm water

½ cup whole milk

1 egg, lightly beaten

2 cups all-purpose flour (maida), plus extra for dusting

1 teaspoon salt

4 tablespoons vegetable oil

Method

- Combine all the spices in a small frying pan and dry-roast over low heat till fragrant. Transfer the roasted spices to a mortar and pestle and grind to a coarse powder.
- For naan, combine yeast with sugar and ½ cup water in a small mixing bowl and mix well. Cover and leave in a warm place for 7 to 10 minutes to allow yeast to froth.
- Meanwhile, combine the remaining water with milk and egg. Whisk well.
- Combine the flour with salt in a large mixing bowl and make a well in the centre. When yeast froths, add to the flour and mix in using your fingertips. Gradually, knead in the milk-egg mixture to make a smooth, soft dough. Transfer the dough onto a lightly-floured surface and knead well for 4 to 5 minutes. Cover with a damp cheesecloth and leave in a warm place for 1 hour, or till dough doubles in volume.
- Add 1 tablespoon of roasted spice mixture to the risen dough and knead lightly. Divide the dough into lime-sized portions and shape each portion into a ball. Place on a lightly-greased baking tray, cover with a damp cheesecloth and leave to ferment for another 30 minutes.
- Preheat oven to 220°C/425°F/Gas 7.
- Roll out the risen dough portions into flat oval naans about 3 inches wide, 6 inches long and ½ inch thick. Brush the naans with oil and sprinkle liberally with spice mixture. Pat down gently so spices adhere to the naans.
- Place the prepared naans on a lightly-greased baking tray and bake in the preheated oven for 3 to 4 minutes till golden and fluffy. Serve hot with raita or curry.

Kachori

Crisp, Spiced Lentil-stuffed Breads

Makes 6 kachoris

The humble kachori differs in form and flavour in every Indian state. I've eaten it as a small teatime snack, for breakfast, and even as chaat. The crisp light pastry makes for an excellent canapé base if used with pâtés and other toppings. This recipe is for the large, flat kachori so popular in Rajasthan and Uttar Pradesh, which is eaten with lentils or chickpea curry.

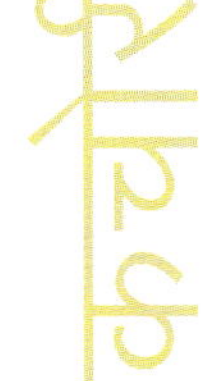

Ingredients

FOR DOUGH

1½ cups all-purpose flour (maida)

¼ teaspoon salt

1 tablespoon clarified butter (ghee)

Vegetable oil for deep-frying

FOR FILLING

1 tablespoon vegetable oil

½ teaspoon asafoetida powder (hing)

1 teaspoon cumin seeds

1 teaspoon fennel seeds (saunf)

1-inch piece ginger, finely grated

1 cup split yellow lentils (moong dal), boiled till tender

2 tablespoons soaked raisins

½ teaspoon sugar

Salt to taste

Method

- Combine the flour with salt in a large mixing bowl. Add clarified butter and crumble it into the flour using your fingertips. Gently knead in just enough water to make a smooth, firm dough. Cover the dough with a damp cheesecloth and set aside.
- To make the filling, heat oil in a large frying pan over medium heat; add asafoetida, cumin and fennel seeds and sauté till they crackle.
- Add ginger, sauté for a minute, then add the remaining ingredients with ¼ cup water. Cook, stirring occasionally, till the mixture dries up and lentils are soft. Crush the lentils slightly with the back of a spoon. Remove from heat and cool to room temperature.
- Divide the dough and cooled filling into 6 equal portions each.
- To shape the kachoris, roll out a portion of dough into a small 2-inch disc. Place a portion of filling in the centre and bring the dough together around the filling, stretching the dough gently to seal the filling inside. Pinch the edges to seal and roll the kachori between your palms gently to give it a good round shape. Repeat with the remaining dough and filling.
- Flatten each kachori gently between your palms and place on a lightly-floured surface. Using a rolling pin, roll out the kachori evenly, to make a 6-inch disc.
- Heat oil in a kadhai over medium heat. Carefully slide in the kachori and deep-fry till golden and crisp. Remove and drain on absorbent paper.
- Serve hot or cool with curry or raita.

NOTE: Kachoris can be stored in a dry, airtight container for up to a week.

Loncha Cha Tandul

Goan Red Rice With Pickling Spices

Serves 4

Ingredients

1 tablespoon vegetable oil

1 teaspoon cumin seeds

1 medium onion, finely sliced

1 heaped tablespoon pickle masala (See page 25)

1½ cups Goan red parboiled rice (ukda chawal) or brown rice, boiled till tender

Salt to taste

A few sprigs fresh coriander, chopped

Of the thousands of varieties of rice grown in India, Goa's parboiled red rice or ukdem tandul is one of the most delicious and nutritious. A bowl of the plump, nutty grains though filling, is light on the stomach, leaving one with a deep sense of satisfaction. The rice needs a long time to cook, so use a pressure cooker to save time.

Method

- Heat oil in a frying pan over medium heat and add cumin seeds.
- When the cumin seeds crackle, add onion and sauté till translucent.
- Add pickle masala, sauté for a couple of seconds and add boiled rice with salt. Toss well to coat rice evenly with spices. Cook till the rice is heated through.
- Sprinkle with coriander and serve hot with yoghurt or raita.

Masala Fugias

मसाला फुगियस

East Indian Spongy Deep-fried Breads

Makes 12 - 15 fugias

Ingredients

2 teaspoons yeast
¼ teaspoon sugar
1¼ cups warm water
2 cups all-purpose flour (maida)
½ teaspoon salt
½ teaspoon white pepper powder
¼ teaspoon dried ginger powder (sonth)
2 medium eggs, lightly beaten
¾ cup whole milk
Vegetable oil for deep-frying

The technique of using yeast for baking bread was brought to India by the Portuguese a few centuries ago. These yeast-leavened fried breads are generally sweetish, but I decided to spice them up a bit, to make an even better accompaniment to the delicious Bombay East Indian curries with which they are usually served.

Method

- In a mixing bowl, combine yeast with sugar and ½ cup warm water and mix well. Cover and leave in a warm place for 5 to 10 minutes to allow yeast to froth.
- Sift flour into a large mixing bowl with salt, white pepper and ginger powder, and make a well in the centre.
- Pour the yeast mixture along with the remaining water into the well and gradually mix with the flour. Add eggs and milk to make a smooth, soft dough. Cover the dough with damp cheesecloth and place the bowl in a warm place for 2 hours, or till the dough rises and doubles in volume.
- Knead the risen dough lightly once again and divide into marble-sized portions.
- Heat oil in a kadhai over medium-low heat. Gently roll the dough portions into balls (fugias) and drop into the oil. Deep-fry, turning the fugias over, till golden. Remove and drain on absorbent paper.
- Serve hot with Grilled Prawns in East Indian Red Coastal Curry (See page 79) or any other spicy curry.

CHUTNEYS AND PICKLES

Tongue ticklers, taste bud stimulants, palate awakeners – pickles and chutneys do more than just accompany a meal. Always playing a supporting role and never the hero, they provide a meal with distinction and attitude. Whether it's perking up a thayir sadam (curd rice, made by mixing cooked rice with yoghurt, salt and a simple tempering of oil, mustard or cumin seeds, green chillies and curry leaves), or jazzing up a pallid khichdi, or even adding some extra oomph to a spicy thepla or biryani, these little flavour bombs are indispensable to an Indian meal. And it is the spices and herbs that give punch to a pickle and chutzpah to a chutney. An Indian meal without a dollop of at least one of these two flavour enhancers will always be lacking.

Jhinga Balchão

Prawn Balchão

झींगा बालचाओ

Makes 1 cup

India is a land of a variety of pickles, each one unique in its own special way. Meat or fish pickles are comparatively rare and are limited to certain regions and communities. Pickled prawns go extremely well with rice or poie (bran bread), the local Goan bread, or mixed with cream cheese, as a surprisingly good topping on crackers for a quick snack.

Ingredients

FOR BALCHÃO SPICE MIX

5 dried Kashmiri chillies

2 tablespoons cumin seeds

1 tablespoon black mustard seeds

½ teaspoon turmeric powder

5 garlic cloves, roughly chopped

1-inch piece ginger, roughly chopped

A pinch of saffron

1 tablespoon sugar

FOR PICKLE

1 large onion, finely sliced

1 teaspoon salt

4 tablespoons vegetable oil

¼ cup brown palm vinegar

1 tablespoon pickle masala (See page 25)

1 cup baby prawns, shelled and deveined

Method

- For balchão spice mix, combine all the ingredients in a blender or processor jar and grind to a smooth paste without adding any water.
- For pickle, heat a frying pan over medium heat; add onion and salt and sauté till the mixture is dry. The salt will cause the onion to release moisture.
- Add oil and sauté till the onion turns brown. Add 1 tablespoon ground balchão spice with vinegar and pickle masala and cook till fragrant.
- Add prawns and toss well. Cook till the prawns are just tender, or for about 1 minute.
- Remove from heat and cool to room temperature. Store for up to a week in a clean, dry jar.

NOTE: The remaining balchão spice mix can be stored and refrigerated for up to 2 weeks. Add a teaspoonful to curries to lend them a spicy zing, or even try pickling other meats or vegetables. It can also be used to stir-fry leftover rice for a quick breakfast or snack.

Ber Ka Achaar

बेर का अचार

Indian Jujube Pickle

Makes about ¾ cup

Ingredients

1 tablespoon vegetable oil

¼ teaspoon asafoetida powder (hing)

1 teaspoon black mustard seeds

1 teaspoon roasted cumin powder

1 teaspoon red chilli powder

½ teaspoon turmeric powder

2 cups Indian jujube (ber), seeded and cut into wedges

Salt to taste

2 teaspoons lime juice

On my way back from school, I invariably bought myself a paper cone filled with boras, as ber are called in Mumbai, sprinkled liberally with salt. I always wondered how they would taste in a pickle. And what would stop me from trying?

Method

- Heat oil in a pan over medium heat and add asafoetida powder and mustard seeds.
- When the spices crackle, add cumin powder, chilli powder and turmeric with the jujubes. Toss well.
- Add salt and cook till the fruits are tender.
- Remove from heat and stir in lime juice.
- Cool to room temperature and transfer to a clean, dry jar. Store for up to a week.

Maas Ka Achaar

Rajasthani Meat Pickle

Makes about 1½ cups

मास का अचार

Ingredients

- 350 g boneless mutton, cut into 2-inch cubes
- 1 cup mustard oil
- 1 tablespoon nigella seeds (kalonji)
- 1 teaspoon asafoetida powder (hing)
- 2 tablespoons pickle masala (See page 25)
- 2 teaspoons salt
- ½ cup vinegar

The Rajputs love meat and find a way of using their favourite food in unique ways such as this meat pickle. Once a traditional travel food for long caravan journeys across the desert; today, this pungent pickled meat is a delicacy that features on festival menus.

Method

- Wash the mutton and pat dry.
- Heat oil in a kadhai over medium heat and add nigella seeds with asafoetida powder.
- When the spices crackle, add the mutton and sauté for 2 to 3 minutes.
- Add pickle masala and salt. Cook, stirring occasionally, till the mutton is done and tender.
- Add vinegar and cook till the mixture is almost dry and the meat is evenly coated with spices.
- Cool to room temperature and transfer to a clean, dry jar. Store for up to 4 weeks.

NOTE: This pickle tastes best when matured for a day or two.

Alsi Ki Chutney

Flaxseed Chutney

Makes about 1 cup

Ingredients

2 cups flaxseed (alsi), lightly roasted

2 teaspoons black pepper powder

1 heaped teaspoon red chilli powder

1½ teaspoons sugar

Salt to taste

Though considered a new-age superfood by western nutritionists, flaxseed or linseed has been consumed in India, particularly Maharashtra, for several centuries. This chutney is simple and delicious, and makes for a great topping on breads and parathas.

Method

- Combine all the ingredients in a grinder or processor jar and grind to a coarse powder.
- Store for up to a month in a clean, dry jar.
- Serve with rotis or sprinkled over naans and kulchas.

Shahtoot Ki Chutney

Ingredients

2 cups fresh mulberries (shahtoot)
1 teaspoon roasted cumin seeds, powdered
½ teaspoon black pepper powder
Salt to taste
½ teaspoon sugar

Mulberry Chutney

Makes about ¾ cup

Memories of stealing mulberries from my neighbour's tree and being given away by the stains on my clothes come alive when I hear the word mulberries. Their tangy flavour coupled with cumin, pepper and sugar in this chutney tempts me to sneak a few berries even today.

Method

- Combine all the ingredients in a frying pan and cook over low heat. Toss the mixture and mash the berries lightly with a fork.
- When the berries are heated through, remove from heat and cool to room temperature.
- Store and refrigerate in a clean, dry jar for up to a week.

Narangi Aur Mosambi Ki Chutney

नारंगी और मोसंबी की चटनी

Orange And Sweet Lime Chutney

Makes about ¾ cup

Ingredients

1 tablespoon vegetable oil
1 teaspoon cumin seeds
1 teaspoon fennel seeds (saunf)
2-inch piece ginger, very finely chopped
4 cloves garlic, very finely chopped
½ cup orange juice
½ cup sweet lime juice
2 tablespoons brown palm vinegar
½ cup sugar
2 large fresh red chillies, sliced
1 teaspoon white pepper powder
Salt to taste
2 oranges (narangi), peeled, segmented and membranes removed
2 sweet limes (mosambi), peeled, segmented and membranes removed

One of the most delicious varieties of orange is grown in Nagpur, the city of oranges. Their sour-sweet flavour combines well with the milder sweet lime, fragrant fennel and spicy chillies to make a lip-smacking accompaniment that will have everyone asking for more.

Method

- Heat oil in a large frying pan over medium heat and add cumin seeds and fennel seeds.
- When the spices crackle, add ginger and garlic and sauté till the ginger softens.
- Stir in orange juice, sweet lime juice and vinegar with sugar and chillies. Bring the mixture to a simmer and cook till the sugar dissolves and chillies soften.
- Add the remaining ingredients and mix gently. Cook till the fruits are slightly tender.
- Remove from heat, cool to room temperature and transfer to a clean, dry jar.
- Store, refrigerated, for up to a week.

RAITAS AND SALADS

Herbs and salads are made for each other. A sprinkling of chopped herbs or lightly toasted spices over raw vegetables, or a crisp salad doused in a tangy herb dressing makes a wonderful palate cleanser - an intermezzo in a lavish meal. A salad can be a simple mélange of chopped raw vegetables, a lush combination of fruit and vegetables enrobed in a creamy dressing, or a cool bowl of yoghurt-drenched ingredients that either complements the main meal or makes a splash on its own. Traditionally, salads were always served chilled or at room temperature, but warm salads are all the rage today.

Anar Aur Pudina Ka Raita

अनार और पुदीना का रायता

Pomegranate, Mint And Yoghurt Salad

Serves 4 - 6

Ingredients

2 cups yoghurt, whisked thick

1 cup fresh pomegranate kernels

1/3 cup fresh mint leaves

1 teaspoon cumin powder

½ teaspoon black pepper powder

1 teaspoon green chilli paste

Salt to taste

Yoghurt is not only cooling and essential for the digestive system, but its tanginess pairs perfectly well with sweet fruits like pomegranate. This raita makes a stunning addition to any dinner table and is a hit among children and adults alike.

Method

- Combine all the ingredients in a bowl and mix well.
- Place in a refrigerator to chill.
- Serve cold with biryani.

Kaleji Ka Raita

Rajasthani Smoked Yoghurt And Liver Salad

Serves 4 - 6

कलेजी का रायता

Ingredients

350 g lamb or goat liver, diced

2 tablespoons mustard oil

1 teaspoon pickle masala (See page 25)

Salt to taste

2 cups yoghurt, whisked thick

1 teaspoon cumin powder

½ teaspoon black pepper powder

A few sprigs fresh mint

FOR SMOKING

2 - 3 pieces charcoal

1 teaspoon vegetable oil

I first ate this dish at a dinner hosted by the Maharaja of Mewar. The idea of using liver in a raita seemed unusual and I was hesitant to try it, but once I did, the smoked yoghurt worked its magic instantly. Here, I've added a new twist to this iconic raita.

Method

- Boil the liver until just cooked through. Drain away the water.
- Heat oil in a frying pan over medium heat. Add the boiled liver with pickle masala and salt. Toss well till heated through and evenly golden. Remove from heat and set aside.
- Heat charcoal on an open flame till red hot. Using tongs, transfer the hot coal to a small metal bowl. Pour yoghurt into a wide bowl and place the metal bowl in the centre. Pour vegetable oil over the coal and as soon as the coal begins to smoke, cover the wider bowl with a tight-fitting lid. Set aside for 6 to 8 minutes.
- When the yoghurt has absorbed the flavour of smoke, remove the metal bowl from yoghurt container and discard the coal.
- Add the cooked liver to the yoghurt with cumin powder, pepper powder and mint. Mix well.
- Serve immediately, sprinkled over with more mint. This raita goes best with rotis or kebabs.

Mishrit Sprout Salad Orange Aur Mirch Ke Mayonnaise Ke Saath

मिश्रित स्प्राउट सलाद ऑरेंज और मिर्च के मेयोनेज के साथ

Mixed Sprout Salad With Orange And Chilli Mayonnaise

Serves 2 - 3

Ingredients

3 cups water

2 cups mixed sprouts

Salt to taste

½ teaspoon fennel seeds (saunf), lightly roasted and powdered

1 large red capsicum, finely chopped

1 large green capsicum, finely chopped

1 large yellow capsicum, finely chopped

½ cup mayonnaise

2 tablespoons orange juice

1 teaspoon red chilli powder

½ teaspoon white pepper powder

In India, we are very lucky to have a wide variety of sprouts available to us. Not only are they very healthy, but they also adapt well to many different and unusual flavours. Here is one such example.

Method

- Combine 3 cups water with ½ teaspoon salt in a saucepan and bring to a rapid boil. Add the mixed sprouts, cook for 30 seconds and drain. Refresh sprouts with cold water and pat dry using a clean kitchen towel.
- In a large mixing bowl, combine sprouts with powdered fennel, red, green and yellow capsicum and toss well. Refrigerate.
- In a small mixing bowl, combine mayonnaise with orange juice, chilli powder and white pepper. Mix well.
- Serve the salad chilled with orange chilli mayonnaise on the side.

Palak Aur Gehun Ka Salad

पालक और गेहूँ का सलाद

Spinach And Wheat Salad

Serves 4

Ingredients

- 1 cup wholewheat grains (gehun), washed and drained
- 2 cups water
- Salt to taste
- 1 tablespoon vegetable oil
- 1 teaspoon red chilli powder
- ½ teaspoon coriander powder
- ½ teaspoon cumin powder
- ¼ teaspoon clove powder
- 2 cups spinach, shredded
- 1 large red onion, roughly sliced
- 1 large tomato, roughly chopped
- 1 large lime

Spinach and wheat are two of the most typecast ingredients in any cuisine. One was rarely eaten raw till recently, and the other is always ground and used in breads. "Why not use them as they are?" I thought. And the answer was this wonderfully light, yet, filling salad.

Method

- Combine wheat grains with 2 cups water and ½ teaspoon salt in a saucepan and bring to a boil over medium heat. Boil the mixture, stirring occasionally, till the wheat is cooked and tender, but, not mushy. Drain extra water and rinse the cooked wheat in cold water.
- In a large bowl, combine oil with powdered spices and mix well.
- Add the cooked wheat, spinach, onion and tomato and toss to mix. Squeeze in lime juice, toss once more and serve.

Bhuna Hua Makai Aur Shimla Mirch Salad

भुना हुआ मकई और शिमला मिर्च सलाद

Tossed Salad With Roasted Corn And Peppers

Serves 4

Ingredients

2 tablespoons olive oil

1 teaspoon garlic paste

Salt to taste

Black pepper powder to taste

¾ teaspoon fennel seeds (saunf), lightly roasted and powdered

½ tablespoon apple cider vinegar

1 cup corn kernels

8 - 10 cherry tomatoes, halved lengthwise

1 large red onion, sliced into rings

1 large green capsicum, cut into large squares

2 oranges, peeled and segments separated

1 small head curly endive lettuce, torn into large pieces

A tossed salad is so common that we seem to take it for granted. This one, however, will definitely grab your attention. By marinating the vegetables in a fragrant marinade and roasting them lightly, this is a tossed salad with an attitude.

Method

- In a large bowl, combine olive oil with garlic paste, salt, pepper, fennel powder and vinegar. Whisk well with a fork.
- Add corn, cherry tomatoes, onion rings, capsicum and toss well. Set aside for 5 minutes.
- Add the orange segments to the vegetables and mix gently.
- Heat a grill pan over medium-high flame. Spoon the marinated vegetables onto the pan and grill, turning regularly till light char marks appear.
- Divide the salad among 4 serving plates and top with lettuce. Serve immediately.

DESSERTS

A meal without a dessert is like a fascinating story with an unsatisfactory, abrupt ending. After a fulfilling repast of savoury dishes, one needs the meal to end on a soaring, sweet note. A good dessert will round off a meal and leave a lingering sweetness on the palate long after the meal is over. A touch of spice to complement and heighten the sweetness will make a dessert more memorable for the delightfully unexpected tingling on the tongue. Cardamoms, cinnamon, cloves and nutmeg have long been dessert-friendly spices, but a dash of chilli or pepper opens up new daring avenues to explore with some exciting results.

Baked Dahi Tartlets

Baked Yoghurt Tartlets

Makes 6 - 8

My first encounter with warm yoghurt was in West Bengal in the form of a classic bhapa doi or sweet steamed yoghurt. Here, I've used the same elements and baked the yoghurt in tartlets. Baking gives the yoghurt a firmer texture, leaving its creaminess intact.

बेक्ड दही टार्टलेट्स

Ingredients

FOR PASTRY

1 cup all-purpose flour (maida), plus extra for dusting

¼ teaspoon coriander powder

1 tablespoon caster sugar

½ cup chilled butter, plus extra for greasing tart moulds

A few drops vanilla essence

1 egg yolk

FOR BAKED YOGHURT

2 cups thick yoghurt

1 cup sweetened condensed milk

1 medium egg, beaten

1 teaspoon milk masala (See page 25), ground to a fine powder

¼ teaspoon dried ginger powder (sonth)

MISCELLANEOUS

6 to 8 tart moulds

Method

- For pastry, sift flour with coriander powder into a large mixing bowl. Add caster sugar and mix well. Add butter with vanilla essence and crumble into the flour using your fingertips.
- Add egg yolk and mix well; bring the mixture together with very little chilled water to make a firm dough. Cover and refrigerate for 10 minutes.
- Meanwhile, grease the tart moulds well with butter. Preheat oven to 180°C/350°F/Gas 4.
- Place the prepared pastry dough on a lightly-floured surface and roll out into a thin sheet, about 1/3 inch thick. Using the rim of a bowl or glass which is double the diameter of the tart mould, cut the pastry into circles. Line the greased tart moulds with pastry and prick all over with a fork.
- For baked yoghurt, whisk all the ingredients together and spoon into pastry-lined tart moulds. Place the moulds on a baking tray and place in the preheated oven.
- Bake for 12 to 15 minutes, or till the pastry is golden and the yoghurt filling has set. To test if done, insert a toothpick into the centre of the yoghurt filling. If done, it should come out clean.
- Remove from the oven and leave aside to cool. Carefully remove from the moulds when cold. Place in a refrigerator and serve chilled.

Dahi Mirch Pepper Cupcakes

Yoghurt Chilli Pepper Cupcakes

Makes 6 cupcakes

दही मिर्च पेपर कपकेक्स

Ingredients

¾ cup whole milk

¼ teaspoon red chilli powder

½ teaspoon black pepper powder

2 cups all-purpose flour (maida)

1 teaspoon baking powder

¾ tablespoon sodium bicarbonate

⅓ cup cocoa powder

1 cup yoghurt, whisked

¾ cup caster sugar

A few drops of vanilla essence

¾ cup white butter

FOR GARNISH

Icing sugar

MISCELLANEOUS

Cupcake moulds

These eggless cupcakes are easy to make and full of spicy surprises. Topped with Philadelphia cheese frosting, they are perfect for a high tea spread.

Method

- Combine milk with chilli powder and pepper powder in a saucepan and bring to a boil over medium heat. As the milk boils, remove from heat and cool to room temperature.
- Preheat oven to 170°C/325°F/Gas 3.
- In a large mixing bowl, sift flour with baking powder, sodium bicarbonate and cocoa powder.
- Add yoghurt with caster sugar, vanilla and white butter. Whisk till smooth and frothy.
- Add small quantities of the flour mixture, alternating with spiced milk and mix to make a smooth, thick batter.
- Pour the batter into the cupcake moulds till three-fourth full. Place the filled cups on a baking tray and bake in the preheated oven for 20 minutes, or till a toothpick inserted in the centre comes out clean.
- Remove from the oven and cool to room temperature. While the cupcakes cool down, dust the surface with icing sugar.
- Serve warm or cooled.

Orange Aur Adrak Mousse

Orange And Ginger Mousse

Serves 4

ऑरेंज और अदरक मूस

Ingredients

3 large egg yolks

½ cup sugar

1 cup warm whole milk

2 teaspoons unflavoured gelatine, soaked in 2 tablespoons warm water

1 cup yoghurt, whisked

Grated rind of 1 orange

½ teaspoon dried ginger powder (sonth)

1 teaspoon fresh ginger juice

½ cup fresh orange juice

1 cup whipped cream

Indian fresh ginger root is sharp and strong and infuses a sweet, spicy flavour to this orange mousse. I've used both the fresh and dried ginger, as I love the different flavour of each one.

Method

- Combine egg yolks with sugar in a mixing bowl and whisk till light and creamy. Whisk in warm milk and place the bowl over a pan of simmering water. Stir with a wooden spoon and cook till the custard thickens and begins to coat the back of the spoon.
- Remove the bowl from heat, add gelatine and stir well till completely dissolved.
- Stir in the remaining ingredients, pour into serving bowls and refrigerate till set. Serve chilled.

Aadu Ke Malpuay

Peach Malpuas

erves 4

Ingredients

FOR MALPUAS

1½ cups all-purpose flour (maida)

¾ cup grated khoya (creamy, coagulated milk solids)

1¼ cups whole milk

½ teaspoon white pepper powder

Clarified butter (ghee) for shallow-frying

2 tablespoons honey

FOR PEACHES

8 canned peach halves

1 teaspoon fennel seeds (saunf)

I look forward to visiting Mohammed Ali Road in Mumbai during the month of Ramadan, mainly to feast on the fresh, sweet malpuas. They pair perfectly with fresh fruit, and here, I have combined them with peaches and fennel seeds to offset their richness.

Method

- For malpuas, whisk flour, khoya, milk and pepper together to make a smooth batter. Cover and set aside for 20 minutes.
- Brush a frying pan liberally with clarified butter and heat over a medium-low heat. Using a spoon, drop some batter in the centre of the pan and spread to make a 4-inch disc. Drizzle clarified butter around the edges and fry till golden on one side. Flip over and drizzle more clarified butter around the edges. Reduce the heat to low and cook till golden on both sides and done. Remove onto a plate. Repeat with the remaining batter.
- Drain the peaches and reserve 1 cup syrup. Cut the peach halves into wedges.
- Combine the peach syrup with fennel seeds in a pan and bring to a boil over medium heat. Add peaches, reduce heat to low and simmer for 2 minutes.
- To serve, place a malpua on each serving plate and brush with honey. Carefully lift a couple of peach wedges and place on the malpua. Cover with another malpua. Repeat to make a stack of 3 malpuas topped with peaches.
- Serve warm.

NOTE: This dessert can also be made using fresh peaches. Substitute the canned peaches with 4 fresh peaches, cut in half and pitted. Cook the peaches with fennel seeds, ½ cup sugar and ½ cup water till tender and the skin begins to peel. Remove the peel before using.

Masaledar Brownies

Spiced Brownies

Serves 4

A midnight snack of brownies and warm milk will provide a whole new comforting experience with this spicy version. Try the recipe with a little white chocolate to make spiced blondies.

मसालेदार ब्राउनीज

Ingredients

- ½ cup Dutch cocoa or any strong cocoa powder
- ½ cup butter, plus extra for greasing baking tray
- 1¼ cups sugar
- 3 large eggs
- A few drops of vanilla essence
- 1 heaped cup all-purpose flour (maida)
- ¼ teaspoon black pepper powder
- ¼ teaspoon dried ginger powder (sonth)
- ¼ teaspoon red chilli powder
- ½ cup broken walnut kernels

Method

- Combine cocoa with butter and sugar in a large mixing bowl and place over a pan of simmering water. Cook, stirring constantly, till the butter melts and the sugar dissolves.
- Whisk the eggs with vanilla essence and fold into cocoa-butter-sugar mixture. Remove the mixture from heat.
- Sift flour with pepper, dried ginger and chilli powder and fold into the cocoa-egg mixture.
- Preheat oven to 180°C/350°F/Gas 4.
- Grease a 6-inch square baking tin and pour the brownie mixture into it. Shake the tray to even out the mixture. Sprinkle over with walnuts, evenly.
- Place in the preheated oven and bake for 30 minutes.
- Serve warm or cooled.

Thandai Soufflé

ठंडाई सूफ्ले

Makes 4 individual soufflés

Who says thandai can only be enjoyed in summers? With this warm soufflé, the heady flavours of thandai can be enjoyed all year long.

Ingredients

½ cup butter, plus 3 tablespoons to grease soufflé moulds
2 tablespoons all-purpose flour (maida)
2 cups hot whole milk
¼ cup caster sugar, plus 2 tablespoons for dusting soufflé moulds
8 medium eggs, separated
2 heaped tablespoons thandai masala (See NOTE below)

MISCELLANEOUS

4 soufflé moulds

Method

- Grease the soufflé moulds liberally with butter and dust evenly with caster sugar. Refrigerate the greased and dusted moulds.
- Melt butter in a saucepan over low heat; add flour and cook till the mixture is fragrant. Whisk in hot milk and bring the mixture to a rapid boil.
- When the mixture thickens slightly, remove from heat, add sugar and stir to dissolve. Cool to room temperature.
- Whisk the egg yolks and thandai masala into the sweet milk and flour mixture (panada).
- Preheat oven to 200°C/400°F/Gas 6.
- Transfer the egg whites to a clean, dry glass bowl and whisk till stiff peaks form.
- Add the stiffly beaten egg whites to the cooked panada and fold gently, but quickly, to mix well.
- Pour the soufflé mixture into chilled moulds till three-fourth full. Place in the preheated oven and bake till the soufflé rises and turns light golden on the surface.
- Remove from oven and serve immediately.

NOTE: Though thandai masala and thandai syrup are easily available in most grocery stores, the home-made version tastes best. Grind ¼ cup blanched, peeled and dried almonds, 2 tablespoons lightly roasted poppy seeds (khus khus), 2 tablespoons melon seeds (char magaz), 1½ tablespoons fennel seeds (saunf), 1 tablespoon black peppercorns, 5 to 6 pods green cardamom and ½ tablespoon dried rose petals to a fine powder. Store in a clean, dry airtight container.

Afterword

Hunger for variety in food comes in various forms. In this age of globalisation, the need for contact with your family, nowadays often living quite far away, affects people of all ages. Ask an Indian, what they could get from back home, most will reply: Spices, pickles, mangoes, sweets ... and the list goes on!!

The longing for food from your native country is a universal phenomenon. Today, this has created a common ground for national culinary traditions. With the world getting smaller by the day, infused flavours coming through cultural exchange, yet still holding onto the individual's own cuisine, has become a common modification.

I have known Michael for a few decades now. His efforts to marry his culinary training and expertise from the west to his roots in India have always been commendable. Simple spices and their blends used to recreate dishes from ingredients readily available in a household have been his art and strength.

Through this book, Michael makes a commendable effort to be true to the subcontinent's authenticity and richness of the spices and blends, with a twist of modernity. He has given his culinary imagination a whole new dimension.

Lord Gulam Kaderbhoy Noon (1936 – 2015)

Acknowledgements

I was never a good student, but, I am grateful to my teachers for instilling in me a love for reading and research. I remember with great affection Mrs. Pinto, Mrs. Mani and Mrs. Bracken of Bombay Scottish School; and Fr. Jerry Rosario of Xavier Institute of Communications (XIC) who taught me a lot about the camera and gave me my first one when I was ten; and the league of photographers, thereafter, who taught and inspired me.

My love of research and learning continues even today, and I am ever grateful for the support I get from fellow chefs including Chef Naren Thimmaiah, Chef Surjan Singh Jolly, Chef Surya Nayak, Chef Gautam Chaudhary, Chef Sabyasachi Gorai, Chef Easo Johnson, Chef Arzooman Irani and Chef Chatursingh Farsvarn to name just a few. No list of thanks in my book will ever be complete without a note of gratitude for Chef Anton Mossiman whose book on his travels to India was an eye-opener for the then-in-college Michael, who was inspired to look at Indian cuisine in a new way, with the hope to earn for its variety and complexity the appreciation and recognition it deserves. And another very special heart-felt gratitude is due to Dr. Manjit Singh Gill, for not only penning the Foreword for this book, but more importantly, for guiding every generation of chefs, added to the fraternity every year, through his books, which became our textbooks!

A big Thank You to my team and associates: Mrunal Savkar and Radhika Agarwal for helping me with the research; Rita D'Souza, who helped shape the manuscript; my publisher and friends at Om Books International — particularly Ajay Mago and Dipa Chaudhuri for their patience and unflinching support, and Shraboni Roy for making this book look so fabulous. Most of all, thanks to my timeless and patient friends Mugdha Savkar and Ganesh Shedge, who put up with my eccentricities in the kitchen, particularly while we were testing the recipes for this book.

Last, but not by far the least, my thanks to Mum and Anju. Mum, for buying me more and more cookbooks to read and absorb, and Anju, for always being there.

Measurement & Temperature

Metric cup & spoon sizes*

cup	**metric**
1/4 cup	60ml/g
1/3 cup	80ml/g
1/2 cup	125ml/g
1 cup	250ml/g
spoon	**metric**
1/4 teaspoon	1.25ml/g
1/2 teaspoon	2.5ml/g
1 teaspoon	5ml/g
2 teaspoons	10ml/g
1 tablespoon (equal to 3 teaspoons)	15ml/g

Celsius (electric)	**Fahrenheit**	**Gas Mark**	
120°	250°	1	very slow
150°	300°	2	slow
160°	325°	3	moderately slow
180°	350°	4	moderate
190°	375°	5	moderately hot
200°	400°	6	hot
230°	450°	7	very hot
250°	500°	9	very hot

INDEX

T

V

W

Y